C·L·A·S·S·I

Monologues
for Men

MONOLOGUES FROM 16TH, 17TH,
AND 18TH CENTURY PLAYS

EDITED BY KYLE DONNELLY

HEINEMANN · PORTSMOUTH, NH

Heinemann Educational Books, Inc.
361 Hanover Street
Portsmouth, New Hampshire 03801-3959

Offices and agents throughout the world

Library of Congress Cataloging-in-Publication Data

Classical monologues for men: monologues from 16th, 17th, and
    18th century plays / edited by Kyle Donnelly.
        p. cm.
    Includes bibliographical references.
    ISBN 0-435-08619-7 : $7.95
        1. English drama--Early modern and Elizabethan, 1500–1600.
    2. English drama--17th century. 3. English drama--18th century.
    4. Monologues. 5. Men--Drama. 6. Acting. I. Donnelly, Kyle.
    PR1245.C47   1992
    822'.04508'0081--dc20   92-29025
                                                                 CIP

Interior and cover design by Tom Allen, Pear Graphic Design
Printed in the United States of America
92 93 94 95 96 9 8 7 6 5 4 3 2 1

Table of Contents

Comic

Serio-Comic

Introduction

I COULDN'T BEGIN TO COUNT the times actors have come up to me and asked, Do you know of any good classical monologues that would be right for me? Finding a good monologue, in any category, is a tricky proposition. Finding one that is not seen repeatedly at auditions is quite difficult. Most theatres, if they've scheduled Shakespeare in their season, or if they regularly do classical or verse plays, want a "classical monologue" as part of their general auditions. Just what is considered a classical monologue? Most actors use, and rightly so, Shakespeare as their classical source. All actors who are interested in pursuing classical work should have a few good Shakespearean monologues under their belt. If you truly have a passion for Iago, Richard II, or Benedick, you must, by all means, study these roles. With any luck, someday, you'll get the chance to do more than audition with their monologues.

But directors are primarily interested in seeing and hearing how you handle verse and elevated language. Does it have to be Shakespeare? I think not. There are some exciting and challenging alternatives.

The wonderful, wide-ranging body of dramatic literature from the sixteenth, seventeenth, and eighteenth centuries is neglected by most American actors. Unfortunately, it is often neglected by most theatre producers as well. Hence, our exposure to this body of work is limited except, perhaps, in certain academic institutions. A notable exception is the Royal Shakespeare Company, and their productions at the Swan Theatre in Stratford. Since 1986, the RSC at Stratford has been, as they state in their programs, "dedicated to the discovery and rediscovery of Shakespeare's context: plays by his contemporaries, plays that influenced him, plays that he influenced, and plays he was rumored to have had a hand in writing." The RSC has helped bring attention to texts that had lapsed into obscurity. I have had the pleasure of directing two such plays, *The Rover*, by Aphra Behn, at the Goodman Theatre in Chicago, and *Hyde Park*, by James Shirley, at the Huntington Theatre in Boston. I discovered them to be eminently playable and delightful audience pleasers. I urge you to open yourself up to these quite unfamiliar works.

This volume of men's monologues includes characters of all types and ages, confronting and wrestling with the social and political mores of the periods represented. In the funny, outrageous category are the notorious fops, including Sir Formal, attempting to wax eloquent on the plight of a mouse in a mousetrap in *The Virtuoso;* Mr. Puff, the self-important theatre critic in *The Critic;* and Sir Harry Flutter describing in great detail his miserable, hungover breakfast with an intolerant wife in *The Discovery.* If you need more dramatic material, either Pandulpho's grieving the loss of his son in *Antonio's Revenge;* or Young Wilmot's recounting the sad tale of his life in *The Fatal Curiosity* may fill the bill. In addition to the more prevalent upper class characters, there is a wide range of servants to choose from: Sosia, stumbling around in the dark in *Amphitryon;* Lopez, an exquisitely sensible coward in *The Mistake;* or Leanchops in *The Projectors.*

The ripest and widest-range of male characters reside in the lovers/lusters, expressing sentiments from the unqualified delight in women expressed by Nymphadoro in *The Fawn,* to the various accusers of whoredom exemplified by Monticelso in *The White Devil.* These men also have their fantasies, dreams and quandaries, as Ramble in *The Country Wit* imagines the lady who has sent for him, and Falorus in *The Obstinate Lady* must decide whether to betray a friend in love. These dreams know no age barrier: the aging Rufaldo looks forward to marrying a young girl in *Love Tricks,* and

Heartwell and Fondlewife experience love throes in spite of their advanced years in *The Old Bachelor.*

So you will find much to choose from here, in both distinct characterization and specific point of view. The range of age, period, and style, allows every actor to find a suitable monologue. If done well, these pieces will let you demonstrate a facility with complicated language, a sense of style, and an adventurous spirit. Directors, especially those looking for classical actors, are delighted to have something "new" to watch and listen to.

But a director wants more than originality of material. Particularly with this kind of material, your most important considerations will be clarity of text, and confident individual interpretation. First, of course, you must understand the text thoroughly and speak it clearly, being sure to allow the poetic element in the writing to soar. Ultimately, however, your individual interpretation is critical to the success of your audition. These plays, especially the comedies, center around the characters. Certainly there are plot twists galore, but generally, it is the individuality of the character, against a backdrop of intrigue or drama, that makes the play touching or humorous. The character names give you an idea of both the specificity and the broad, bold strokes used by the playwright in depicting the characters themselves — Lord Wronglove, Sir Formal, Fondlewife, Ramble, Suckdry, Mr. Puff. But it is the actor who can bring his individuality to the characterization who will create a living, breathing character, rather than a museum piece.

What practical steps can you take to handle these unfamiliar, and not always easily understandable texts? First, and most importantly, you must *read the play.* You cannot hope to create a complex character if you do not know the context of the monologue. It has been said many times before, and cannot be said enough: Read the play. Consult the bibliography at the back of the volume, and then go to your local university library. You should be able to find many, if not all, of these plays there.

Next, it is important to acknowledge the difficulty of understanding the text on a first reading. The plots are often quite complicated, and the language, in both usage and structure, can be quite unfamiliar. I have often had to read these plays many times, keeping one finger on the character breakdown, in order to keep straight who's who, and who's doing what, or who wants to do what with (or to) whom. So don't feel mentally deficient if it takes you extra time and effort to get it.

The third important step in working on these monologues is to understand what you are saying. This sounds obvious, but it is a basic problem, and often one an actor neglects in his initial work on the text. When in doubt at all about context, go back to the original play. Look up unfamiliar words, preferably in an Oxford English Dictionary, which will give original references and ancient definitions. Look up familiar words if they're used in an unfamiliar context. You may discover something about that word you never knew before. If a passage is particularly complicated, try breaking the sentences down grammatically. Most importantly, don't assume or generalize. The more specific your meaning, the clearer and more interesting your characterization — and the moments that build it — will be, both for you and for your audience.

Fourth, change what doesn't work for you. A monologue must be able to stand on its own, apart from the play. We have chosen beginnings, middles, and ends of speeches; in some cases, we've cut and pieced several speeches together. If you find that beginning or ending your monologue of choice in a different spot, or making a few internal cuts works better for you, more power to you. The versions here are certainly not set in stone. You might also change a piece by taking out obscure references or changing extremely difficult or obtuse words that sound odd to modern ears. However, be careful not to sanitize the work. Even though your audience may not know exactly what a reference means, the sound of the words may convey a particular tone or specific sensibility. And don't forget that it is part of the actor's art to be able to convey a context that will give a word meaning.

After choosing the piece, doing your homework, and getting it up on its feet, consider a test-run for your monologue. Try it out on someone who has not been privy to any of your process, not necessarily for formal criticism, but for feedback on the clarity and effectiveness of your work. Did he understand what you were saying? Did she get a sense of the character without knowing the play, or the period? Were you believable? Getting the reaction of someone you trust might help you to clarify sections you have inadvertently skimmed over or neglected.

Auditioning is rarely easy, but give yourself credit for choosing a classical audition piece not seen by every director hundreds of times. I can speak only for myself, but as a director who has sat through many an audition, good and bad, I certainly appreciate the change of pace.

Kyle Donnelly

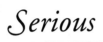

Serious

The Adventures of Five Hours

Don Carlos: I find your travels, cousin, have not cur'd you
  Of that innate severity to women,
  Urg'd justly as a national reproach
  To all of us abroad. The rest o' th' world
  Lament that tender sex amongst us here,
  Born only to be honorable prisoners;
  The greater quality, the closer kept:
  Which cruelty is revenged upon ourselves,
  Whilst, by immuring those whom most we love,
  We sing and sigh only to iron gates.
  As cruel is that overcautious custom
  By proxy to contract parties unknown
  To one another; this is only fit
  For sovereign princes, whose high qualities
  Will not allow of previous interviews:
  They sacrifice their love to public good,
  Consulting interest of state and blood;
  A custom which as yet I never knew
  Us'd amongst persons of a lower rank
  Without a sequel of sad accidents.
  Sir, understand me right; I speak not this
  By way of prophecy: I am not stranger
  To Don Antonio's reputation,
  Which I believe so just, I no way doubt
  Your sister's being happy in him.

Alcibiades

Thomas Otway   *Act I; Serious*

Tissiphernes: Ungrateful king! Thy shallow aims pursue,
But my brisk upstart favorite, have at you.
Was it for this my active youth I spent
In war? And knew no dwelling but a tent?
Have I for this through envious mountains passed,
Demolished cities, and lay'd kingdoms waste?
Still in his cause unwearied courage shown,
And almost hid his head in Crowns I won?
Upon my breast received so many scars
They seem a war described in characters?
And must the harvest of my toil and blood
Upon a fawning rebel be bestowed?
Who, having false to his own country been
Comes here to play his treasons o'er again?
Must he at last tumble my trophies down
And revel in the glories I have won?
Whilst from my honors, they me disengage
With a dull compliment to feeble age.
What ails this hardy hand, that yet it should
Tremble at death, or start at reeking blood?
Methinks this dagger I as firmly hold
And with a strength as resolute and bold
As he who kindly would its point impart
A present to an envied Favorite's heart;
And I, fond youth, will try to work thy fall,
Though with my own I crown thy funeral.
Envy and malice from your mansions fly,
Resign your horror and your snakes to me,
For I'll act mischiefs yet to you unknown;
Nay, you shall all be saints when I come down.

Alcibiades

Thomas Otway   *Act II, scene i; Serious*

Tissaphernes: Now all is ripe, methinks I see
   Treason walk hand in hand with Destiny,
   And both in a kind aspect smile on me.
   Now the whole court proceeds to solemnize
   The Nuptials of proud Alcibiades.
   Where ev'rything does as I'd wish combine,
   To give a happy end to my design.
   It is our custom at a marriage feast,
   The bridegroom —
   With a full bowl presents his chiefest guest.
   The cups, by my greatest secrecy and care,
   With strongest poison all infected are:
   Which when our Alcibiades shall bring
   And offer as his duty to the king,
   The poison and his sudden death will seem
   Full a traitrous design in him.
   Then must the crown descend on me, and so
   I feast my rage, and my Ambition, too.
   Let cowards' spirits start at cruelty,
   Remorse has still a stranger been to me.
   I can look on their pains with the same eyes
   As priests behold the falling sacrifice.
   Whilst they yell out the horror of their moans,
   My heart shall dance to the music of their groans.

All Mistaken, or, The Mad Couple

James Howard *Act I, scene i; Serious*

Duke: She's gone, and after her my heart is flown,
  'Tis well it has no tongue to make its moan;
  Then 'twould discover what my pride conceals,
  A heart in love (though slighted) love reveals.
  Yet though I love her still, she shall not know;
  Her hate shall seem my joy, which is my woe.
  My constancy I'll outwardly disguise,
  Though here within I am not half so wise.
  Yet rather than disclose my doating fate,
  I'll wound my heart by counterfeiting hate.
  To whine, it would the worst of follies prove,
  Since women only pity when they love.
  With how much scorn she gave me welcome home,
  Ortellus in her hand, to show my doom!
  Me and my triumphs she did so despise,
  As though they'd been unworthy in her eyes.
  'Tis well to her I show'd as much disdain;
  I'd rather perish than she guess my pain.
  But, O, the horrid act she makes me do,
  To fool a woman that is young and true!
  So damn'd a sin, that hell could not invent,
  It is too foul for any punishment;
  To question those above I am afraid,
  Else I would ask them, why they woman made.

Antonio's Revenge

John Marston   *Act I, scene ii; Serious*

Pandulpho: Why, wherefore, should I weep?
  Come, sit, kind nephew; come on; thou and I
  Will talk as chorus to this tragedy.
  He was the very hope of Italy,
  The blooming honor of my drooping age.
  They say men of hope are crush'd,
  Good are suppress'd by base desertless clods,
  That stifle gasping virtue. Look, sweet youth,
  How provident our quick Venetians are
  Lest hooves of jades should trample on my boy;
  Look how they lift him up to eminence,
  Heave him 'bove reach of flesh.
  Would'st have me cry, run raving up and down
  For my son's loss? Would'st have me turn rank mad,
  Or wring my face with mimic action,
  Stamp, curse, weep, rage, and then my bosom strike?
  Away, 'tis apish action, player-like.
  If he is guiltless, why should tears be spent?
  Thrice blessed soul that dieth innocent.
  If he is leper'd with so foul a guilt,
  Why should a sigh be lent, a tear be spilt?
  Listen, young blood, 'tis not true valor's pride
  To swagger, quarrel, swear, stamp, rave, and chide,
  To stab in fume of blood, to keep loud coil,
  To bandy factions in domestic broils,
  To dare the act of sins whose filth excels
  The blackest customs of blind infidels.
  No, my lov'd youth, he may of valor vaunt
  Whom fortune's loudest thunder cannot daunt,
  Whom fretful galls of chance, stern fortune's siege
  Makes not his reason slink, the soul's fair liege,

Whose well peis'd action ever rests upon
Not giddy humors, but discretion.
This heart in valor even Jove out-goes;
Jove is without, but this 'bove sense of woes;
And such a one, eternity.

The Brothers

James Shirley *Act III, scene i; Serious*

Fernando: Yes, Francisco,
  He hath left his curse upon me.
  His curse. Dost comprehend what that word carries,
  Shot from a father's angry breath? Unless
  I tear poor Felisarda from my heart,
  He hath pronounced me heir to all his curses.
  Does this fright thee, Francisco? Thou hast cause
  To dance in soul for this, 'tis only I
  Must lose and mourn. Thou shalt have all, I am
  Degraded from my birth, while he affects
  Thy forward youth, and only calls thee son,
  Son of his active spirit, and applauds
  Thy progress with Jacinta, in whose smiles
  Thou mayest see all thy wishes waiting for thee,
  Whilst poor Fernando, for her sake, must stand
  An excommunicate from every blessing,
  A thing that dare not give myself a name,
  But flung into the world's necessities,
  Until in time, with wonder of my wants,
  I turn a ragged statue, on whose forehead
  Each clown may carve his motto.

A Cure for a Cuckold

John Webster   *Act I, scene i; Serious*

Lessingham: By your favor,
  For as I ever to this present hour
  Have studied your observance, so from henceforth
  I now will study plainness — I have loved you
  Beyond myself, mis-spent for your sake
  Many a fair hour, which might have been employed
  To pleasure, or to profit, have neglected
  Duty to them from whom my being came,
  My parents; but my hopeful studies most.
  I have stolen time from all my choice delights,
  And robbed myself thinking to enrich you.
  Matches I have had offered, some have told me,
  As fair, as rich — I never thought 'em so,
  And lost all these in hope to find out you,
  Resolve me, then, for Christian charity.
  Think you an answer of that frozen nature
  Is a sufficient satisfaction for
  So many more than needful services?
  Whence might this distaste arise?
  Be at least so kind to perfect me in that:
  Is it some dislike lately conceived
  Of this my person, which perhaps may grow
  From calumny and scandal? If not that,
  Some late received melancholy in you?
  If neither, your perverse and peevish will —
  To which I most imply it?
  Oh, name it, Sweet.
  I am already in a labyrinth
  Until you guide me out.

Cutter of Coleman Street

Abraham Cowley   *Act I, scene i; Serious*

Truman Junior: How hard, alas, is that young lover's fate,
Who has a father covetous and choleric!
What has he made me swear?
I dare not think upon the oath, lest I should keep it —
Never to see my mistress more, or hear her speak
Without his leave; and farewell then the use
Of eyes and ears; —
And all this wickedness, I submitted to,
For fear of being disinherited;
For fear of losing dirt and dross, I lose
My mistress — there's a lover! Fitter much
For hell than thousand perjuries could make him;
Fit to be made th'example which all women
Should reproach men with, when themselves grow false;
Yet she, the good and charitable Lucia,
With such a bounty as has only been
Practiced by heaven, and kings inspired from thence,
Forgives still, and still loves her perjured rebel.
I'll to my father straight and swear to him
Ten thousand oaths ne'er to observe that wicked one
Which he has extorted from me — Here he comes;
And my weak heart, already used to falsehood,
Begins to waver.

Every Man in his Humor

Ben Jonson   *Act II, scene iii; Serious*

Kno'well: Believe me, I am taken with some wonder,
   To think, a fellow of thy outward presence
   Should, in the frame and fashion of his mind,
   Be so degenerate, and sordid-base!
   Art thou a man? And sham'st thou not to beg?
   To practice such a servile kind of life?
   Why, were thy education ne'er so mean,
   Having thy limbs, a thousand fairer courses
   Offer themselves to thy election.
   Either the wars might still supply thy wants,
   Or service of some virtuous gentleman,
   Or honest labor; nay, what can I name,
   But would become thee better than to beg?
   But men of thy condition feed on sloth,
   As doth the beetle on the dung she breeds in,
   Not caring how the mettle of your minds
   Is eaten with the rust of idleness.
   Now, afore God, whate'er he be, that should
   Relieve a person of thy quality,
   While thou insist'st in this loose desperate course,
   I would esteem the sin not thine, but his.

Fatal Curiosity

George Lillo   Act I, scene iii; Serious

Young Wilmot: Oh, Eustace, Eustace!
Thou knowest, for I've confessed to thee, I love.
But, having never seen the charming maid,
Thou canst not know the fierceness of my flame.
My hopes and fears, like the tempestuous seas
That we have passed, now mount me to the skies,
Now hurl me down from that stupendous height
And drive me to the center. Did you know
How much depends on this important hour,
You would not be surprised to see me thus.
The sinking fortune of our ancient house,
Which time and various accidents had wasted,
Compelled me young to leave my native country,
My weeping parents, and my lovely Charlot,
Who ruled and must forever rule my fate.
How I've improved, by care and honest commerce,
My little stock, you are in part a witness.
'Tis now seven tedious years since I set forth
And, as th'uncertain course of my affairs
Bore me from place to place, I quickly lost
The means of corresponding with my friends.
Oh, should my Charlot, doubtful of my truth
Or in despair ever to see me more,
Have given herself to some more happy lover!
Distraction's in the thought! Or should my parents,
Grieved for my absence and oppressed with want,
Have sunk beneath their burden and expired,
While I, too late, was flying to relieve them,
The end of all my long and weary travels,
The hope, that made success itself a blessing,
Being defeated and forever lost,

What were the riches of the world to me?
I doubt, but I despair not. No, my friend,
My hopes are strong and lively as my fears,
And give me such a prospect of my happiness
As nothing but fruition can exceed.
They tell me Charlot is as true as fair,
As good as wise, as passionate as chaste;
That she, with fierce impatience like my own,
Laments our long and painful separation;
That we shall meet, never to part again;
That I shall see my parents, kiss their tears
From their pale hollow cheeks, cheer their sad hearts,
And drive that gaping phantom, meager want,
Forever from their board, crown all their days
To come with peace, with pleasure, and abundance,
Receive their fond embraces and their blessings,
And be a blessing to 'em.

The Fawn

John Marston   *Act I, scene ii; Serious*

Hercules: Amazed, even lost in wond'ring, I rest full
  Of covetous expectation: I am left
  As on a rock, from whence I may discern
  The giddy sea of humor flow beneath,
  Upon whose back the vainer bubbles float
  And forthwith break. O mighty flattery,
  Thou easiest, common'st, and most grateful venom
  That poisons courts and all societies,
  How grateful dost though make me! Should one rail
  And come to sear a vice, beware leg-rings
  And the turned key on thee, when, if softer hand
  Suppling a sore that itches (which should smart) —
  Free speech gains foes, base fawnings steal the heart.
  Swell, you impostumed members, till you burst;
  Since 'tis in vain to hinder, on I'll thrust,
  And when in shame you fall, I'll laugh you from hence,
  And cry, "So end all desperate impudence."
  Another's court shall show me where and how
  Vice may be cured; for now beside myself,
  Possessed with almost frenzy, from strong fervor
  I know I shall produce things mere divine:
  Without immoderate heat, no virtues shine.
  For I speak strong, though strange: the dews that steep
  Our souls in deepest thoughts are fury, and sleep.

The Fleire

Lord Piso: Still tongueless night, put off thy sable robe,
Thou needs not mourn, my villainies were done
By day, thou hadst no hand in them.
Oh, I am great as is a woman that is near her time,
And life's the burden that I bear.
But 'tis a bastard for that I am ashamed on't.
The law I hope is a skillful midwife, and will soon deliver me.
Grim Justice, do thy worst.
Thy cruelty shall prove a courtesy,
And bail me out of prison.
Lie there, thou self consuming taper, true pattern of my life,
I have consumed myself for others, as thou hast done for me,
And now she has extinguished my life as I this light.
O, how obedient was my bounty still
To her command? My liberality
Did fatten mischief, and hath made her proud.
Oh, that too much of any thing should be so ill in every thing.
The sun's all seeing eye, with too much intemperate heat
Makes wither what it made to flourish.
The earth being mother to all wholesome herbs,
With too much fatness oft produceth weeds.
A suit of cloth doth keep the body warm,
When richer garments make the wearer proud.
O, the mean's the sweetest music;
Contentment revels when that string is touched;
But oh, the time will come she will repent
My death. For when she looks on vice's face
Unmasked like mine, she will detest and loath it.
For this is truth, and evermore hath been,
None can forsake before he knows his sin.

The Ladies of Castile

Mercy Otis Warren   *Act I, scene iv; Serious*

Don Juan de Padilla: I have beheld the ruins of a queen,
   A sight too piteous for a soldier's eye—
   Whose heart, unsteel'd by scenes of human woe,
   Has yet a tender corner left for grief.
   Rob'd of her crown, authority, and peace—
   Dethron'd, immur'd, neglected by her son,
   Shut up in window'd solitude to weep
   Ungrateful Philip, who despis'd her charms,
   She's but the weeping image of despair.
   She, all attentive, listen'd to the tale;
   And rous'd at once as from lethargic dreams,
   And starting, cried "Is Ferdinand no more!
   Is that great monarch slumbering in the tomb
   While I, a wretched prisoner of state
   Stand the sad monument of human ills?"
   She wept and sigh'd, till strong resentment rose
   And kindled in her breast a noble flame.
   With all the powers of eloquence and truth
   I strove to sooth her wandering mind to rest.
   In justice's sacred name I urg'd her aid
   To counteract the cruelties of Charles,
   To reassume her rights, and reign again,
   To extricate her subjects from despair —
   She gave assent with dignity and ease,
   And, spite of nature, seem'd to be a queen.
   I nam'd Calabria's injur'd noble prince,
   The heir of Aragon, long since depriv'd
   Of his paternal crown, and princely rights,
   Which Ferdinand, by violence, had seiz'd,
   And justice bade his daughter to restore;
   I urg'd her marriage with so brave a prince,

Entitled, both by virtue and by blood,
To wield the scepter that his fathers won,
And shield her person from all future wrongs;
But naming love, her dormant passions wak'd,
And kindled up her former flame for Philip;
She sank despondent, and refus'd aid
To act in council or to guide the realm . . .
Haste to Maria, whose undaunted soul
Reflects a luster on her feeble sex;
 By stratagem, she's gained an ample sum
To quiet mutiny, and pay the troops.
But ere the solemn midnight clock shall strike,
Return, and meet me at the gate of Toro.

Love Tricks

James Shirley   *Act II, scene ii; Serious*

Cornelio: Selina, thou know'st I am thy father.
And you know you have rejected young Infortunio.
And you know what man
He is with whom you mean to tie that knot
Nothing but death is able to undo:
Rufaldo, an old man.
Oh, Selina!
Felice, thy poor sister, thou recall'st
To sad remembrance; but heaven, alas!
Knows only where she is.
Thou, with thy uncle's tenderness, wast kept
Always in the country, not, until her loss,
At home with me: her fate taught me to give
A liberty to thee; her I restrain'd,
Poor wench, in love with Gasparo, till, betwixt
Obedience to a father, and the love
To him, she left us both, father and friend.
Now, to avoid the like affliction,
I vow'd thy freedom; and thou see'st I do not
Encounter thy affection with the bonds
A father might enforce upon his child.
But yet, Selina
Take heed, be not too rash; I have observed
You want no common judgment; O, do not
Precipitate thyself into a sorrow
Shall waste thee with repentance; let me tell you,
There is a method, when your passion's young,
To keep it in obedience: you love Rufaldo!
Are thou not young? How will the rose agree
With a dead hyacinth? or the honey woodbine
Circling a withered briar? —

You can apply. Can you submit your body
To bed with ice and snow, your blood to mingle?
Would you be deaf'd with coughing, teach your eye
How to be rheumatic? Breathes he not out
His body in diseases, and like dust,
Falling all into pieces, as if nature
Would make him his own grave. I say too much.
Oh, what are all the riches of the world
To an oppressed mind, which then must be
Fed with despair of change? or will his gold
Buy off th'imprisonment? Nay, will it not
Compose the chains, that bind you to endure it?
Well, I have said enough, keep still your freedom —
And lose it where you will, you shall not blame
Me for your fate, nor grieve me with your shame.

Love Tricks

James Shirley   *Act IV, scene ii; Serious*

Infortunio: A prey! A prey! Where did you get that face?
That goddess' face? It was Selina's once;
How came you by it? Did she, on her death bed
Bequeath her beauty as a legacy,
Not willing it should die, but live and be
A lasting death to Infortunio?
Oh, she was cruel, not to bury it with her!
But I'm a fool! 'Tis Venus and her son —
Where be your bow and arrows, little Cupid?
Didst thou maliciously spend all thy quiver
Upon my heart, and not reserve one shaft
To make Selina love me? Tell me, Venus,
Why did you use me so? You shall no more
Be queen of love. Stay, stay, Cupid was blind,
How comes he now to see? Yes, he did see,
He never could have wounded me so right else.
Why, then let Fortune have her eyes again,
And all things see how wretched I am made.
Ha! Do you know Selina? She is married to
Rufaldo, the old usurer, that went
To bed afore to his money, and begat
Forty in the hundred. Now he beds Selina,
And lays his rude hand o'er her sacred breast,
Embraceth her fair body; now he dares
Kiss her, and suck ambrosia from her lip.
Those eyes that grace the day, now shine on him,
He her Endymion, she his silver Moon.
The tongue that's able to rock Heaven asleep,
And make the music of the spheres stand still
To listen to the happier airs it makes
And mend their tunes by it; that voice is now

Devoted to his ears, those cheeks, those hands
Would make gods proud to touch, are by his touch
Profaned every hour. Oh, this makes me mad!
But I will fit them for it, for I'll die;
It may be then she'll weep, and let fall tears
Upon my grave stone, which shall be of marble,
And hard like her, that if she pour out floods,
No drops shall sink through it, to soften me.
I will be wrapped in lead to keep out prayers,
For then, I know, she'll beg I would be friends.
But then I will be just, and hate her love,
As she did mine, and laugh to see her grieve.

The New Inn

Ben Jonson   *Act I, scene vi; Serious*

Lovel: Oh, thereon hangs a history, mine host.
Did you ever know, or hear, of the Lord Beaufort,
Who served so bravely in France? I was his page,
And, ere he died, his friend. I followed him,
First i' the wars, and i' the time of peace,
I waited on his studies: which were right.
He had no Arthurs, nor no Rosicleers,
No Knights o' the Sun, nor Amadis de Gauls,
Primaleons, and Pantagruels, public nothings;
Abortives of the fabulous, dark cloister,
Sent out to poison courts and infest manners:
But great Achilles, Agamemnon's acts,
Sage Nestor's counsels, and Ulysses' sleights,
Tydides' fortitude, as Homer wrought them
In his immortal fancy, for examples
Of the heroic virtue. Or, as Virgil,
That master of the epic poem, limned
Pious Aeneas, his religious prince,
Bearing his aged parent on his shoulders,
Rapt from the flames of Troy, with his young son!
And these he brought to practice, and to use.
He gave me first my breeding, I acknowledge,
Then showered his bounties on me, like the Hours,
That open handed sit upon the clouds,
And press the liberality of heaven
Down to the laps of thankful men! But then,
The trust committed to me, at his death,
Was above all! And left so strong a tie
On all my powers as time shall not dissolve,
Till it dissolve itself, and bury all —
The care of his brave heir, and only son!

Who, being a virtuous, sweet, young, hopeful lord,
Hath cast his first affections on this lady.
And though I know, and may presume her such,
As, out of humor, will return no love;
And therefore might indifferently be made
The courting-stock, for all to practice on,
As she doth practice on us all, to scorn:
Yet, out of a religion to my charge,
And debt professed, I ha' made a self-decree,
Ne'er to express my person, though my passion
Burn me to cinders.

The Obstinate Lady

Sir Aston Cokain   *Act V, scene iii; Serious*

Falorus: What will become of me, unfortunate man,
Who needs must live in fire or live in shame?
I know not what to speak, nor what to do,
Both fear and grief do so confound my senses.
I fear to wrong Carionil so much
As to be traitorous against our friendship;
And griefs unsufferable ensure for the
Fairest of ladies, incomparable Lucora.
I would she had been kind unto my friend;
Unto him, them, I never had prov'd false.
Nor will I. I will rather search out frozen
Climates, and lie whole nights on hills of ice,
Or rather will take powerful potions and sleep
Out these unpleasant hours I have to live;
But then I shall not see that beauty. Who
But senseless frantics would have thoughts so poor?
My reason forsakes the government of this
Weak frame, and I am fall'n into disorder.
Oh, I could sigh my body into air,
And weep't it into a lake, if merciless nature
Had made it of a substance suitable
Unto my wish now! Methinks I could level
A promontory into a province, and tread
The center through to read the destinies
Of southern stars, and bless their fortunes that
Are born under their light, for I am confident
Their influences are more mild than ours.
There is no other fate can fall on me
Shall awe me now; I will be proud and daring,
As the ambitious waves, when wrathful blasts
Of northern winds do hoist them violently

Against the highest clouds, and rather will
Destroy myself than wrong Carionil.

The Ordinary

William Cartwright   *Act I, scene i; Serious*

Meanwell: My father still
  Runs in my mind, meets all my thoughts, and doth
  Mingle himself in all my cogitations.
  Thus to see eager villains drag along
  Him unto whom they crouched! to see him haled
  That ne'er knew what compulsion was, but when
  His virtues did incite him to good deeds,
  And keep my sword dry! O unequal nature!
  Why was I made so patient as to view
  And not so strong as to redeem? Why should I
  Dare to behold, and yet not dare to rescue?
  Had I been destitute of weapons, yet
  Armed only with the name of son, I might
  Have outdone wonder. Naked piety
  Dares more than fury well appointed; blood
  Being never better sacrificed than when
  It flows to him that gave it. But alas,
  The envy of my fortune did allow
  That only which she could not take away —
  Compassion, that which was not in those savage
  And knowing beasts, those engines of the law
  That even killed as uncontrolled as that.
  How do I grieve when I consider from
  What hands he suffered. Hands that do excuse
  The indulgent prison, shackles being here
  A kind of rescue. Young man, tis not well
  To see thy aged father thus confin'd.
  Good, good old man! Alas! Thou'rt dead to me,
  Dead to the world, and only living to
  That which is more than death, thy misery!
  The grave could be a comfort, and shall I —

O would this soul of mine — But death's the wish
Of him that fears; he's lazy that would die,
I'll live, and see that thing of wealth, that worm
Bred out of splendid muck, that citizen,
Like his own sullied wares, thrown by into
Some unregarded corner; and my piety
Shall be as famous as his avarice.
His son, whom we have in our tuition
Shall be the subject of my good revenge:
I'll count myself no child, till I have done
Something that's worth the name. My brain shall be
Busy in his undoing; and I will
Plot ruin with religion. His disgrace
Shall be my zeal's contrivement; and when this
Shall style me son again, I hope 'twill be
Counted not wrong, but duty. When that time
Shall give my actions growth, I will cast off
This brood of vipers, and will show that I
Do hate the poison which I meant to apply.

Oroonoko

Oroonoko: There was a stranger in my father's court
Valued and honored much. He was a white,
The first I ever saw of your complexion.
He changed his gods for ours and so grew great;
Of many virtues and so famed in arms
He still commanded all my father's wars.
I was bred under him. One fatal day,
The armies joining, he before me stepped,
Receiving in his breast a poisoned dart
Levelled at me; he died within my arms.
He left an only daughter, whom he brought
An infant to Angola. When I came
Back to the court a happy conqueror,
Humanity obliged me to condole
With this sad virgin for a father's loss,
Lost for my safety. I presented her
With all the staves of battle to atone
Her father's ghost. But when I saw her face
And heard her speak, I offered up myself
To be the sacrifice. She bowed and blushed;
I wondered, and adored. The sacred pow'r
That had subdued me then inspired my tongue,
Inclined her heart, and all our talk was love.
      O! I was too happy.
I married her. And though my country's custom
Indulged the privilege of many wives,
I swore myself never to know but her.
She grew with child, and I grew happier still.
O my Imoinda! But it could not last.
Her fatal beauty reached my father's ears.
He sent for her to court, where, cursed court!

No woman comes but for his amorous use.
He raging to possess her, she was forced
To own herself my wife. The furious king
Started at incest. But grown desperate,
Not daring to enjoy what he desired,
In mad revenge, which I could never learn,
He poisoned her, or sent her far, far, off,
Far from my hopes ever to see her more.

Pizarro

Richard Brinsley Sheridan   *Act II, scene ii; Serious*

Rolla: Yet never was the hour of peril near, when to inspire them words were so little needed. My brave associates — partners of my toil, my feelings, and my fame! — can Rolla's words add vigor to the virtuous energies which inspire your hearts? No — you have judged as I have, the foulness of the crafty plea by which these bold invaders would delude you — Your wondrous spirit has compared as mine has, the motives which, in a war like this, can animate their minds, and ours. They, by a strange frenzy driven, fight for power, for plunder, and extended rule — We, for our country, our altars, and our homes. — They follow an adventurer whom they fear, and obey a power which they hate. We serve a monarch whom we love, a God whom we adore. Whene'er they move in anger, desolation tracks their progress! Where'er they pause in amity, affliction mourns their friendship! They boast, they come but to improve our state, enlarge our thoughts, and free us from the yoke of error! Yes, they will give enlightened freedom to our minds, who are themselves the slaves of passion, avarice, and pride. They offer us their protection — Yes, such protection as vultures give to lambs — covering and devouring them! They call on us to barter all of good we have inherited and proved, for the desperate chance of something better which they promise. Be our plain answer this: the throne we honor is the people's choice — the laws we reverence are our brave fathers' legacy — the faith we follow teaches us to live in bonds of charity with all mankind, and die with hope of bliss beyond the grave. Tell your invaders this, and tell them, too, we seek no change; and least of all, such change as they would bring us.

The Relapse

Sir John Vanbrugh   *Act III, scene ii; Serious*

Loveless: Sure fate has yet some business to be done
   Before Amanda's heart and mine must rest.
   Else why, amongst those legions of her sex
   Which throng the world
   Should she pick out for her companion
   The only one on earth
   Whom nature has endowed for her undoing?
   Undoing, was't I said? Who shall undo her?
   Is not her empire fixed? Am I not hers?
   Did she not rescue me, a groveling slave,
   When chained and bound by that black tyrant Vice
   I labored in his vilest drudgery?
   Did she not ransom me and set me free?
   Nay more, when by my follies sunk
   To a poor, tattered, despicable beggar,
   Did she not lift me up to envied fortune,
   Give me herself, and all that she possessed
   Without a thought of more return
   Than what a poor repenting heart might make her?
   Han't she done this? And if she has,
   Am I not strongly bound to love her for it?
   To love her! Why, do I not love her, then?
   By heaven and earth, I do.
   Nay, I have demonstration that I do:
   For I would sacrifice my life to serve her.
   Yet hold. If laying down my life
   Be demonstration of my love,
   What is't I feel in favor of Berinthia?
   For should she be in danger, methinks I could incline
   To risk it for her service, too; and yet I do not love her.
   How then subsists my proof?

Oh, I have found it out.

What I would do for one is demonstration of my love, and if I'd do as much for t'other, it there is a demonstration of my friendship. Ay — so it must be so. I find I'm very much her friend. Yet let me ask myself one puzzling question more: whence springs this mighty friendship all at once? For our acquaintance is of later date. Now friendship's said to be a plant of tedious growth, its root composed of tender fibers, nice in their taste, cautious in spreading, checked with the least corruption in the soil, long ere it take and longer still ere it appear to do so; whilst mine is in a moment shot so high and fixed so fast, it seems beyond the power of storms to shake it. I doubt it thrives too fast.

The Sack of Rome

Mercy Otis Warren

Gaudentius: Was this the dowry of the fair Eudocia,
   The mangl'd body of my much lov'd sire
   Presented by her father's guilty hand?
   Just gods avenge — the trait'rous deed avenge!
   What is the faith — or what the gratitude,
   Or what the sacred promise of an Emperor?
   As cruelty portrays an abject mind,
   Servility precedes the fall of states
   In this declension of the Roman world,
   While tyrants dip their scimitars in blood,
   And sport on human misery at large,
   Shall I sit down with folded arms and see
   A monster gorging on a parent's blood;
   Or unavenging behold a father die
   By Valentinian's base ungrateful hand?
   Yet he, alas, is my Eudocia's sire:
   But glory, fame, ambition, and revenge
   Bid me erase this passion from my heart
   And boldly stem the madness of the times,
   Recover Rome and reinstate her power,
   And bring her back to glory, wealth, and fame.
   But, ah! Eudocia, pensive and alone;
   Shall I advance, or banish her forever?
   One tear dissolves the firmness of my soul,
   Unmans the mind, and lets the warrior down;
   Dashes his hope, and weakens his resolve;
   'Tis ruin to retire — death to speak.
   Chaste as Diana in each graceful move,
   While Venus lights the features of her face
   And gives her son the torch to fire my soul;
   Yet honor, conscience, virtue, and the world

Forbid a union with his bloody house;
My father's murderer — the gods forbid!
Yet she's all innocence — and virtue's soul
Shines forth conspicuous in her heavenly form.
I haste from her as from the hand of death.

The Sack of Rome

Mercy Otis Warren   *Act III, scene i; Serious*

Maximus: Tortures may seize, furies tear my heart
But words can't utter what my soul endures;
Confusion darkens all my powers of speech,
And blushes blast the wretch that sacrificed
His fame - his peace - his honor - and his wife
To glut a tyrant's lust. My brain grows hot —
It kindles to distraction — Yet Valentinian lives.
She, ever duteous to her lord's command,
Was, by the darkest plot of hell, deceived.
This ring, so often by her husband sent
In times too dangerous for other message,
To her presented, by the base Heraclius,
Reluctantly, she hastened to the palace —
Though terror seized and chilled her frighted soul;
She through each hollow, vacant room was drag'd,
Till in the silent deep abode of guilt,
As a dark fiend, the emperor alone
Waited the victim of his madden'd flame.
He seized his prey — nor cries nor tears avail'd;
She Heaven implored — to pitying angels pray'd,
And in despair, she call'd on her Petronius
Yet thought his sanction back'd the vile design.
Twas past midnight when I return'd
With anxious dread and deep suspense I flew
To her abode of misery and grief.
In sables dressed, a taper just burnt down,
That darkly glimmer'd gloom from side to side —
Indignant scorn glanc'd from her languid eye;
While tears bedew'd her bright angelic face,
As if a cherub wept, the radiant beams
Of stars obscur'd, or of extinguish'd suns;

Dismay'd, she held a dagger in her hand
As half resolved to plunge it in her breast,
Yet trembled at the purpose of her soul;
I caught her hand, and drew the weapon thence,
Ere she perceive'd her wretched husband nigh.
"Poor Maximus" she cried, "Spite of thy guilt,
My soul pities thee — receive this pledge
To cheat some other soft, believing fool;
Blot from thy thought that e'er Ardelia liv'd
To be the sport of riot and debauch."
Then fix'd the fatal signet on my hand,
This curs'd signet that has sealed my doom,
And branded me with infamy forever.
She breathed a sob as if a seraph sighed,
Drop'd a kind tear, and smiled a last adieu.
All the big passions of a noble soul
Thrilled through her heart, and stiffened all her frame;
The shining angel left this blasted world
And now, methinks, ineffably serene,
On yon bright azure cloud,
Ardelia gently chides this tardy hand
That lingers thus while unavenged her death,
Her soul unstain'd, immaculate and pure.
Not meager malice dare impeach her mind;
Nor e'en Megara's tongue, though it were dipped
In all the poisons of her curling snakes,
Till the gall ganger'd every name but hers,
Durst whisper aught to wound Ardelia's fame.
But yet her wrongs may urge this dauntless arm
And give full vigor to a bold design,
To smite a sceptered brow — yes — that is all —
The man himself's a poltroon —
Yet he's an emperor.
Go, find my friends, and ere the work begins,
I ask a moment to indulge my grief;
The luxury of tears is not for me —

My soul's too big for such a soft relief;
Yet I may rave and riot o'er my woes.

The Sack of Rome

Mercy Otis Warren   *Act IV, scene i; Serious*

Maximus: Now what am I? An emperor. A splendid wretch
Perched on the blood stained summit of the world.
Search through each horrid wild of dreary woe,
From Tiber's stream to Danube's frozen banks,
From fair Hetruria to the Hyrcanian wood,
Or blacker forests of Carpathian gloom.
There's not a culprit so completely cursed,
Tortured in pomp, in tenfold misery plunged
And torn with guilty greatness as myself.
Happy Damocles — only envied king
Whose reign began and ended in a day!
My vengeance now's complete; but where's my peace?
Oh! Could I leave the world of Roman slaves
Exiled to Italy's most distant bounds,
Resume that life of innocence and ease
Which blessed the noontide of my happier days,
When my Ardelia's smile crowned all my bliss!
But, ah! her name —
Wakes all the baleful passions of my soul.
If Valentinian's grim and ghastly ghost
Still wanders here, and can be more accursed,
Let mad Alecto's furious sisters join
To make his woes complete — and doubly damned,
Let him look through the dank and dismal shades
Of night and death — in anguish let him see
His rival riot in Eudocia's arms.

Two Noble Kinsmen

William Shakespeare & John Fletcher   *Act II, scene ii; Serious*

Arcite: Banished the kingdom? 'Tis a benefit,
    A mercy I must thank 'em for; but banished
    The free enjoying of that face I die for,
    O, 'twas a studied punishment, a death
    Beyond imagination; such a vengeance
    That, were I old and wicked, all my sins
    Could never pluck upon me. Palamon,
    Thou hast the start now; thou shalt stay and see
    Her bright eyes break each morning 'gainst thy window,
    And let in life into thee; thou shalt feed
    Upon the sweetness of a noble beauty
    That Nature ne'er exceeded, nor ne'er shall.
    Good gods, what happiness has Palamon!
    Twenty to one, he'll come to speak to her,
    And if she be as gentle as she's fair,
    I know she's his; he has a tongue will tame
    Tempests, and make the wild rocks wanton.
    Come what can come,
    The worst is death; I will not leave the kingdom.
    I know mine own is but a heap of ruins,
    And no redress there. If I go, he has her.
    I am resolved another shape shall make me,
    Or end my fortunes. Either way, I am happy;
    I'll see her, and be near her, or no more.

Two Noble Kinsmen

William Shakespeare & John Fletcher   *Act II, scene i; Serious*

Palamon: O, cousin Arcite,
  Where is Thebes now? Where is our noble country?
  Where are our friends and kindreds? Never more
  Must we behold those comforts, never see
  The hardy youths strive for the games of honor,
  Hung with the painted favors of their ladies,
  Like tall ships under sail; then start amongst 'em
  And, as an east wind, leave 'em all behind us,
  Like lazy clouds, whilst Palamon and Arcite,
  Even in the wagging of a wanton leg,
  Outstripped the people's praises, won the garlands,
  Ere they have time to wish 'em ours. O, never
  Shall we two exercise, like twins of honor,
  Our arms again, and feel our fiery horses
  Like proud seas under us! Our good swords now —
  Better the red-eyed god of war ne'er wore —
  Ravished our sides, like age must run to rust,
  And deck the temples of those gods that hate us;
  These hands shall never draw 'em out like lightning
  To blast whole armies more.

Venice Preserv'd

Thomas Otway   *Act I, scene i; Serious*

Priuli: Have you not wrong'd me?
  Yes, wrong'd me, in the nicest point:
  The honor of my house; you have done me wrong;
  You may remember (for I now will speak,
  And urge its baseness:) When you first came home
  From travel, with such hopes, as made you looked on
  By all men's eyes, a youth of expectation;
  Pleased with your growing virtue, I received you;
  Courted, and sought to raise you to your merits:
  My house, my table, nay, my fortune, too,
  My very self, was yours; you might have used me
  To your best service; like an open friend,
  I treated, trusted you, and thought you mine;
  When in requital of my best endeavors,
  You treacherously practiced to undo me,
  Seduc'd the weakness of my age's darling,
  My only child, and stole her from my bosom:
  You stole her from me, like a thief, you stole her,
  At dead of night, that cursed hour you chose
  To rifle me of all my heart held dear.
  May all your joys in her prove false like mine;
  A sterile fortune, and a barren bed
  Attend you both: Continual discord make
  Your days and nights bitter and grievous: Still
  May the hard hand of a vexatious need
  Oppress and grind you; till at last you find
  The curse of disobedience all your portion.

Venice Preserv'd

Thomas Otway   *Act I, scene i; Serious*

Jaffeir: My lord, my lord; I'm not that abject wretch
You think me. Patience! Where's the distance throws
Me back so far, but I may boldly speak
In right, though proud oppression will not hear me!
Could my nature e'er
Have brook'd injustice or the doing wrongs,
I need not now thus low have bent myself,
To gain a hearing from a cruel father!
Wrong'd you? 'Tis to me you owe her,
Childless you had been else, and in the grave,
Your name extinct, nor no more Priuli heard of.
You may remember, scarce five years are past,
Since in your brigantine, you sailed to see
The Adriatic wedded by our Duke,
And I was with you. Your unskillful pilot
Dash't us upon a rock; when to your boat
You made for safety, entered first yourself;
The affrighted Belvidera following next,
As she stood trembling on the vessel side,
Was by a wave wash't off into the deep,
When instantly, I plunged into the sea,
And buffeting the billows to her rescue,
Redeem'd her life with half the loss of mine;
Like a rich conquest in one hand I bore her,
And with the other dashed the saucy waves
That thronged and pressed to rob me of my prize:
I brought her, gave her to your despairing arms:
Indeed you thanked me, but a nobler gratitude
Rose in her soul: for from that hour she loved me,
Till for her life she paid me with her self.

The White Devil

Flamineo: Now, you that stand so much upon your honor,
    Is this a fitting time o' night, think you,
    To send a duke home without e'er a man?
    I would fain know where lies the mass of wealth
    Which you have hoarded for my maintenance,
    That I may bear my beard out of the level
    Of my lord's stirrup. Pray, what means have you
    To keep me from the galleys, or the fallows?
    My father prov'd himself a gentleman,
    Sold all's land, and like a fortunate fellow,
    Died ere the money was spent. You brought me up,
    At Padua, I confess, where, I protest,
    For want of means (the university judge me),
    I have been fain to heel my tutor's stockings
    At least seven years. Conspiring with a beard
    Made me a graduate, then to this Duke's service;
    I visited the court, whence I returned
    More courteous, more lecherous by far,
    But not a suit the richer. And shall I,
    Having a path so open, and so free
    To my preferment, still retain your milk
    In my pale forehead? No, this face of mine
    I'll arm and fortify with lusty wine
    'Gainst shame and blushing.
    I would the common'st courtesan in Rome
    Had been my mother than thyself.
    Nature is very pitiful to whores
    To give them but few children, yet those children
    Plurality of fathers; they are sure
    They shall not want. Go, go,
    Complain unto my great lord cardinal,

Yet may be he will justify the act.
Lycurgus wondered much men would provide
Good stallions for their mares, and yet would suffer
Their fair wives to be barren.

The White Devil

John Webster　　　　　　　　　　　　*Act III, scene ii; Serious*

Monticelso: Observe this creature here, my honored lords,
　　A woman of a most prodigious spirit
　　In her effected.
　　You see, my lords, what good fruit she seems,
　　Yet like those apples that travelers report
　　To grow where Sodom and Gomorrah stood
　　I will but touch her and you straight shall see
　　She'll fall to soot and ashes.
　　Were there a second paradise to lose
　　This devil would betray it.
　　Who knows not how, when several night by night
　　Her gates were choked with coaches, and her room
　　Outbrav'd the stars with several kind of lights
　　When she did counterfeit a prince's court?
　　In music, banquets and most riotous surfeits
　　This whore, forsooth, was holy.
　　Shall I expound whore to you? Sure I shall;
　　I'll give their perfect character. They are first
　　Sweetmeats which rot the eater: in man's nostril
　　Poison'd perfumes. They are coz'ning alchemy,
　　Shipwracks in calmest weather! What are whores?
　　Cold Russian winters, that appear so barren,
　　As if that nature had forgot the spring.
　　They are the true material fire of hell,
　　Worse than those tributes in th' Low Countries paid,
　　Exactions upon meat, drink, garment, sleep;
　　Ay, even on man's perdition, his sin.
　　They are those brittle evidences of law
　　Which forfeit all a wretched man's estate
　　For leaving out one syllable. What are whores?
　　They are those flattering bells have all one tune,

At weddings, and at funerals: you rich whores
Are only treasuries by extortion fill'd,
And emptied by curs'd riot. They are worse,
Worse than dead bodies, which are begg'd at gallows
And wrought upon by surgeons, to teach man
Wherein he is imperfect. What's a whore?
She's like the guilty counterfeited coin
Which whosoe'er first stamps it brings in trouble
All that receive it.

The White Devil

John Webster   *Act IV, scene i; Serious*

Francisco: Dearly, sir, I thank you;
   If you ask for me at court, report
   You have left me in the company of knaves.
   I gather now by this, some cunning fellow
   That's my lord's officer, one that lately skipp'd
   From a clerk's desk up to a justice's chair,
   Hath made this knavish summons, and intends,
   As th'Irish rebels wont were to sell heads,
   So to make prize of these. And thus it happens,
   Your poor rogues pay for't, which have not the means
   To present bribe in fist: the rest o' the band
   And raz'd out of the knaves' record; or else
   My lord he winks at them with easy will,
   His man grows rich, the knaves are knaves still.
   But to the use I'll make of it; it shall serve
   To point me out a list of murderers,
   Agents for any villainy. Did I want
   Ten leash of courtesans, it would furnish me;
   Nay, laundress three armies. That in so little paper
   Should lie th'undoing of so many men!
   'Tis not so big as twenty declarations.
   See the corrupted use some make of books:
   Divinity, wrested by some factious blood,
   Draws swords, swells battles, and o'erthrows all good.
   To fashion my revenge more seriously,
   Let me remember my dead sister's face:
   Call for her picture; no, I'll close mine eyes,
   And in a melancholic thought I'll frame
   Her figure 'fore me. Now I ha't — how strong
   Imagination works! How can she frame
   Things which are not! Methinks she stands afore me;

And by the quick idea of my mind,
Were my skill pregnant, I could draw her picture. Did ever
Man dream awake till now? — Remove this object,
Out of my brain with't: what have I to do with tombs, or
death-beds, funerals, or tears,
That have to mediate upon revenge?
So now 'tis ended, like an old wives' story.
Statesmen think often they see stranger sights
Than madmen. Come, to this weighty business.
My tragedy must have some idle mirth in't,
Else it will never pass. I am in love,
In love with Corombona, and my suit
Thus halts to her in verse — [He writes]
I have done it rarely: O, the fate of princes!
I am so us'd to frequent flattery,
That being alone I now flatter myself;
But it will serve; 'tis seal'd. [Enter Servant]
                                        Bear this
To th'house of convertites; and watch your leisure.
To give it to the hands of Corombona,
Or to the matron, when some followers
Of Brachiano may be by. Away! [Servant exits]
He that deals all by strength, his wit is shallow:
When a man's head goes through, each limb will follow.
The engine for my business, bold Count Lodowick —
'Tis gold must such an instrument procure:
With empty fist no man doth falcons lure.
Brachiano, I am now fit for thy encounter.
Like the wild Irish, I'll ne'er think thee dead,
Till I can play at football with thy head.

Comic

Amphitryon

John Dryden   *Act II, scene i; Comic*

Sosia [with a lamp]: Was not the Devil in my Master, to send
me out in this dreadful dark night, to bring the news of his
victory to my lady? And was not I possessed with ten devils,
for going on his errand, without a convoy for the safeguard of
my person? Lord, how am I melted into sweat with fear! I am
diminished of my natural weight, above two stone. I shall not
bring half my self home again to my poor wife and family. I
have been in an ague fit, ever since shut of evening, what
with the sight of trees by the highway, which looked maliciously like thieves by moon-shine, and what with bulrushes
by the riverside, that shake like spears and lances at me. Well!
The greatest plague of a serving-man is to be hired by some
great lord! They care not what drudgery they put upon us,
while they lie lolling at their ease a-bed, and stretch their lazy
limbs in expectation of the whore which we are fetching for
them. The better sort of 'em will say Upon my Honor at
every word; yet ask 'em for our wages, and they plead the
privilege of their honor, and will not pay us, nor let us take
out privilege of the law upon them. There's conscience for
you! Stay — methinks this should be our house, and I should
thank the gods, now, for bringing me safe home, but I think I
had as good let my devotions alone, till I have got the reward
for my good news, and then thank 'em once for all, for if I
praise 'em before I am safe within doors, some damned mas-
tiff dog may come out and worry me; and then my thanks are
thrown away upon them. Now am I to give my lady an
account of my Lord's victory; 'tis good to exercise my parts
before hand, and file my tongue into eloquent expressions, to
tickle her ladyship's imagination. [Setting down his lantern]
This lantern, for once, shall be my lady, because she is the
lamp of all beauty and perfection. Then thus I make my

addresses to her: [Bows] Madam, my lord has chosen me out, as the most faithful, though the most unworthy of his followers, to bring your ladyship this following account of our glorious expedition. Then she: — "Oh, my poor Sosia [in a shrill tone] "how am I overjoyed to see thee!" — She can say no less — "Madam, you do me too much honor, and the World will envy me this glory." — Well answered on my side. — "And how does my lord Amphitryon?" — "Madam, he always does like a man of courage, when he is called by honor." — There I think I nicked it. — "But when will he return?" — "As soon as he possibly can, but not so soon as his impatient heart could wish him with your ladyship." — "But what does he do, and what does he say? Prithee tell me something more of him." — "He always says less than he does, madam, and his enemies have found it to their cost." — Where the devil did I learn all these elegancies and gallantries? How now? What, do my eyes dazzle or is my dark lantern false to me? Is not that a giant before our door? Or a ghost of somebody slain in the late battle? If he be, 'tis unconscionably done, to fright an honest man thus, who never drew weapon wrathfully in all my life! —- Whatever wight he be, I am devilishly afraid, that's certain. But 'tis discretion to keep my own counsel. I'll sing that I may seem valiant.

The Country Wit

John Crowne *Act III, scene i; Comic*

Ramble: Ten thousand thanks, my dear. Sent for by a young handsome lady (so her instrument says she is) to supply not only the absence, but defects of a husband. Well, I am a catholic man of strange universal use, I ought to have a pension for the public service I do the state; but though I am an excellent subject, I am a traitorous lover; how like a barbarous villain do I use that divine creature, Mrs. Christina? If I were fifty Rambles bound together, I had not merit enough for her love; and I, though I am but one, yet parcel my self out every minute to fifty women; yet 'tis not for want of love to her, for the enjoyment of other women gives me not so much delight as a smile from her: and yet, egad, the enjoyment of her would not keep me from the chase of other women. Here am I, raving mad after a woman, only tickled with an image in my own fancy, of a young, pretty, melting, twining, burning creature, who for ought I know may be only an old, ugly, lecherous succuba, like a burning hill, with snow on her top, and fire in her guts, and has enchanted me to her embraces with a delicate young amorous picture, put in my head: no, no, it cannot be; if she were ugly, she would not have the impudence to send for me; nay, she would not have the impudence to love; no, no, she must be handsome, aye, and extremely handsome, too. Let me see, what kind of woman may she be? She has a large, rolling, smiling, black eye, full of fire; a round sweet juicy melting lip, full of blood; even small ivory teeth; full round white hard breasts; a small straight delicate shape; a white little hand, inclining to be moist; a neat little foot; her stature middling — Ay, this is she, I know her as well as if I were married to her: I am sure 'tis she. Egad, I am passionately in love with her. Oh, my dear envoy, come back quickly with full commission from thy lady, or I shall fall into a fever.

The Country Wit

John Crowne *Act IV, scene iii; Comic*

Ramble: Into what a villainous trap I am fallen, dull rogue that I
was, not to know Isabella's voice, where were my ears, my
senses? They were all in my pocket, I was tickled with my
ravishing expectations into a perfect numbness to death. Now
I am discovered in all my rogueries, and intrigues, and false-
hoods, and must never hope to enjoy the sweet pleasure of
lying or forswearing any more. I must now either repent, and
become a downright plodding lover to Christina, or in plain
terms, lose her. I must either forsake all the world for her, or
her for all the world. Well, if I do forsake her, she has this to
boast, I do not forsake her for any one woman, I forsake her
for ten thousand. But what do I talk of forsaking her, will she
not forsake me, after this discovery? And besides her own
anger, will not Sir Thomas compel her? For he is horribly
provoked against me, whatever the matter is. Well, I cannot
bear the loss of Mrs. Christina, I had rather endure marriage
with her than enjoy any other woman at pleasure. I must,
and will repent, and reform, and now should an angel appear
in female shape, he should not tempt me to revolt any more.
[Enter Merry] Oh, Merry, I am ruined. Thou hast undone
me, seduced me from the ways of virtue and constancy, just
as I was entering into 'em. I am not able to resist the tempta-
tion of this plot, but how shall I manage it? For I can no
more make the picture of a face than I can make a face; I
have not so much skill as a man may learn out of the
Compleat Gentleman, and other elaborate pieces that teach
that faculty. Glowing with extreme appetite to her, my
tongue and brain over-heated with motion, in the stream and
whirlpool of thought and babble, I very impudently invited
her to sit to me for her picture, and the foolish cuckold her
husband did accordingly bring her, and leave her with me,

where, when I had squeez'd his orange, I gave him the rind again, and requited him with the shadow of it, drawn by one that could perform it. Come along, Merry, thou must help in this business. Well, I must turn thee away before thy wicked councils have undone me.

The Constant Couple

George Farquhar   *Act V, scene i; Comic*

Sir Harry [Aside]: This is the first whore in heroics that I have
met with. [Aloud] Look ye, madam, as to that slander particular of your virtue, we sha'n't quarrel about it; you may be as
virtuous as any woman in England, if you please; you may
say your prayers all the time. But pray, Madam, be pleased to
consider what is this same virtue that you make such a
mighty noise about. Can your virtue bespeak you a front row
in the boxes? No; for the players can't live upon virtue. Can
your virtue keep you a coach and six? No, no, your virtuous
women walk a-foot. Can your virtue hire you a pew in
church? Why, the very sexton will tell you, no. Can your
virtue stake for you at picquet? No. Then what business has a
woman with virtue? Come, come, madam, I offered you fifty
guineas; there's a hundred. — The devil! Virtuous still! Why,
'tis a hundred, five score, a hundred guineas! Affront! 'Sdeath,
madam! A hundred guineas will set you up at basset, a hundred guineas will furnish out your lodgings with china; a
hundred guineas will give you an air of quality; a hundred
guineas will buy you a rich escritoire for your billets-doux, or
a fine Common-Prayer-Book for your virtue. A hundred
guineas will buy a hundred fine things, and fine things are for
fine ladies, and fine ladies are for fine gentlemen; and fine
gentlemen are for — Egad, this burgundy makes a man speak
like an angel. Come, come, madam, take it and put it to what
use you please.

The Contrast

Royall Tyler   *Act II, scene ii; Comic*

Jessamy: I say there can be no doubt that the brilliancy of your merit will secure you a favorable reception. Say to her! Why, my dear friend, though I admire your profound knowledge of every other subject, yet, you will pardon my saying that your want of opportunity has made the female heart escape the poignancy of your penetration. Say to her! Why, when a man goes a-courting, and hopes for success, he must begin with doing, and not saying. When you are introduced, you must make five or six elegant bows. Then you must press and kiss her hand; then press and kiss, and so on to her lips and cheeks; then talk as much as you can about hearts, darts, flames, nectar, and ambrosia — the more incoherent, the better. If she should pretend — please to observe, Mr. Jonathan — if she should pretend to be offended, you must —- But I'll tell you how my master acted in such a case. He was seated by a young lady of eighteen upon a sofa, plucking with a wanton hand the blooming sweets of youth and beauty. When the lady thought it necessary to check his ardor, she called up a frown upon her lovely face, so irresistibly alluring, that it would have warmed the frozen bosom of age; remember, said she, putting her delicate arms upon his, remember your character and my honor. My master instantly dropped upon his knees, with eyes swimming with love, cheeks glowing with desire, and in he gentlest modulation of voice, he said, My dear Caroline, in a few months our hands will be indissolubly united at the altar; our hearts I feel are already so; the favors you now grant as evidence of your affection are favors indeed; yet, when the ceremony is once past, what will now be received with rapture will then be attributed to duty. The consequence? Ah, forgive me, my dear friend, but you New England gentlemen have such a laudable curiosity of seeing the bottom of everything; — Why, to be honest, I confess I saw the blooming cherub of a consequence smiling in its angelic mother's arms about ten months afterwards.

The Double-Dealer

William Congreve   *Act III, scene i; Comic*

Maskwell: I know what she means by toying away an hour well
enough. Pox, I have lost all appetite to her; yet she's a fine
woman, and I lov'd her once. But I don't know, since I have
been in a great measure kept by her, the case is alter'd; what
was my pleasure is become my duty: And I have as little
stomach to her now as if I were her Husband. Should she
smoke my design upon Cynthia, I were in a fine pickle. She
has a damn'd penetrating head, and knows how to interpret a
Coldness the right way; therefore I must dissemble Ardor and
Ecstasie, that's resolv'd. How easily and pleasantly is that dis-
sembled before fruition! Pox on't that a man can't drink without quenching his thirst. Ha! Yonder comes Mellefont
thoughtful. Let me think. Meet her at eight —- hum — ha!
By Heaven, I have it! if I can speak to my Lord before —
Was it my brain or providence? No matter which — I will
deceive 'em all, and yet secure myself, 'twas a lucky thought!
Well, this Double-Dealing is a jewel.

The Double-Dealer

William Congreve   *Act I, scene i; Comic*

Mellefont: You shall judge whether I have not reason to be alarm'd. None besides you and Maskwell are acquainted with the secret of my Aunt Touchwood's violent Passion for me. Since my first refusal of her Addresses, she has endeavour'd to do me all ill Offices with my Uncle; yet has manag'd 'em with that subtlety, that to him they have worn the face of kindness; while her Malice, like a dark lanthorn, only shone upon me where it was directed. Still, it gave me less perplexity to prevent the success of her displeasure than to avoid the importunities of her Love, and of two evils, I thought myself favour'd in her aversion. But whether urged by her despair and the short prospect of time she saw to accomplish her designs; whether the hopes of her revenge, or of her Love, terminated in the view of this my marriage with Cynthia, I know not, but she surpris'd me in my Bed. What follow'd at first amaz'd me, for I looked to have seen her in all the transports of a slighted and revengeful Woman. But when I expected Thunder from her Voice and Lightning in her Eyes, I saw her melted into Tears, and hush'd into a Sigh. It was long before either of us spoke; Passion had ty'd her Tongue, and Amazement mine. — In short, the Consequence was thus, she omitted nothing that the most violent Love could urge, or tender words express; which when she saw had no effect, but still I pleaded Honor and nearness of blood to my Uncle, then came the storm I fear'd at first. For, starting from my Bed-side like a Fury, she flew to my sword, and with much ado I prevented her doing me or herself a mischief. Having disarm'd her, in a gust of Passion she left me, and in a resolution confirm'd by a Thousand Curses, not to close her Eyes till she had seen my Ruin.

The Discovery

Frances Sheridan   *Act I, scene ii; Comic*

Sir Harry Flutter: Upon my soul, my lord, I have been so
stunn'd this morning with the din of conjugal interrogatories,
that I am quite bated — do, let me lounge a little on this
couch of yours. I came home at three o'clock, as I told you, a
little tipsy, too, by the by, but what was that to her, you
know, for I am always good humored in my cups. To bed I
crept, as softly as a mouse, for I had no more thought of
quarreling with her then, than I have now with your lordship.
—La, says she, with a great heavy sigh, It is a sad thing that
one must be disturbed in this manner; and on she went, mutter, mutter, mutter, for a quarter of an hour, I all the while
lying quiet as a lamb, without making her a word of answers.
At last, quite tired of her perpetual buzzing in my ear,
Prithee, be quiet, Mrs. Wasp, says I, and let me sleep (I was
not thoroughly awake when I spoke). Do so, Mr. Drone,
grumbled she, and gave a great flounce. I said no more, for in
two minutes I was as fast as a top. Just now, when I came
down to breakfast, she was seated at the tea table all alone,
and looked so neat, and so cool, and so pretty, that, e'gad,
not thinking of what had passed, I was going to give her a
kiss; when up she tossed her demure little face. You were a
pretty fellow last night, Sir Harry, says she. So I am every
night, I hope, Ma'am, says I, making her a low bow. Was not
that something in your manner, my lord? — Pray where were
you till that unconscionable hour, says she? At the tavern
drinking, says I, very civilly. And who was with you, Sir? Oh,
thought I, I'll match you in your enquiries; I named your
lordship, and half a dozen more wild fellows (whom, by the
way, I had not so much as seen), and two or three girls of the
town, added I, whistling, and looking another way. Down she
slapped her cup and saucer. If this be the case, Sir Harry (half

sobbing), I shall desire a separate bed. That's as I please, Madam, sticking my hand in my side and looking her full in the face. No, it shall be as I please, sir. — It shan't Madam; It shall, Sir; and it shan't and it shall, and it shall and it shan't, was bandied backwards and forwards till we were both out of breath and passion. At last she said something to provoke me, I don't know what it was, but I answered her a little tartly. You would not have said it, I believe — I'd give the world for your command of temper — but it slipped out, faith, for she vexed me cursedly, I said — faith, I think I — as good as told her she lied. She burst out a-crying, I kick'd down the tea-table, and away I scampered up to your lordship, to receive advice and consolation.

Every Man in His Humor

Ben Jonson   *Act IV, scene iii; Comic*

Brainworm: You should rather ask, where they found me, sir,
for, I'll be sworn I was going along in the street, thinking
nothing, when, of a sudden, a voice calls, "Master Kno'well's
man!"; another cries, "Soldier!": and thus, half a dozen of
'em, till they had called me within a house where I no sooner
came, but they seemed men, and out flew all their rapiers at
my bosom, with some three or fourscore oaths to accompany
'em, and all to tell me, I was but a dead man, if I did not
confess where you were, and how I was employed, and about
what; which, when they could not get out of me — as I
protest, they must ha' dissected and made an anatomy o' me
first, and so I told 'em — they locked me up into a room i'
the top of a high house, whence, by great miracle, having a
light heart, I slid down, by a bottom of packthread, into the
street, and so 'scaped. But, sir, thus much I can assure you,
for I heard it, while I was locked up, there were a great many
rich merchants, and brave citizens' wives with 'em at a feast,
and your son, Master Edward, withdrew with one of 'em,
and has pointed to meet her anon, at one Cob's house, a
water-bearer, that dwells by the wall. Now, there, your worship shall be sure to take him, for there he preys, and fail he
will not.

The Fawn

John Marston   *Act III, scene i; Comic*

Nymphadoro: Faith, Fawn, 'tis my humor, the natural sin of my
sanguine complexion: I am most enforcedly in love with all
women, almost affecting them all with an equal flame. If she
be a virgin of a modest eye, shamefaced, temperate aspect,
her very modesty inflames me, her sober blushes fire me; if I
behold a wanton, pretty, courtly, petulant ape, I am extremely
in love with her, because she is not clownishly rude, and that
she assures her lover of no ignorant, dull, unmoving Venus;
be she sourly severe, I think she wittily counterfeits, and I
love her for her wit; if she be learned and censures poets, I
love her soul, and for her soul, her body; if she be a lady of
professed ignorance, oh, I am infinitely taken with her simplicity, as one assured to find no sophistication about her; be
she slender and lean, she's the Greek's delight, be she thick
and plump, she's the Italian's pleasure; if she be tall, she's of a
goodly form, and will print a fair proportion in a large bed; if
she be short and low, she's nimbly delightful, and ordinarily
quick-witted; be she young, she's for mine eye, be she old,
she's for my discourse, as one well knowing there's much ami-
ableness in a grave matron; but be she young or old, lean, fat,
short, tall, white, red, brown, nay, even black, my discourse
shall find reason to love her, if my means may procure opportunity to enjoy her.

The Fawn

John Marston   *Act II, scene i; Comic*

Hercules: Why should any woman only love any one man, since it is reasonable women should affect all perfection, but all perfection never rests in one man; many men have many virtues, but ladies should love many virtues; therefore ladies should love many men. For as in women, so in men, some woman hath only a good eye, one can discourse beautifully (if she do not laugh), one's well favored to her nose, another hath only a good brow, t'other a plump lip, a third only holds beauty to the teeth, and there the soil alters; some peradventure, hold good to the breast, and then downward turn like the dreamt of image, whose head was gold, breast silver, thighs iron, and all beneath clay and earth; one only winks eloquently, another only kisses well, t'other only talks well, a fourth only lies well. So in men: one gallant has only a good face, another has only a grave methodical beard and is a notable wise fellow (until he speaks), a third only makes water well (and that's a good provoking quality), one only swears well, another only speaks well, a third only does well — all in their kind good; goodness is to be affected; therefore, they. It is a base thing, and indeed an impossible, for a worthy mind to be contented with the whole world, but most vile and abject to be satisfied with one point or prick of the world.

The Grateful Servant

James Shirley   Act III, scene iv; Comic

Grimundo: You know I have given you many precepts of honesty. I have made tedious discourses of heaven to you, and the moral virtues; numbered up the duties of a good prince; urged examples of virtues, for your imitation, reproved you, nay sometimes made complaints of you to the duke. Alas, my lord, I durst do no otherwise. Was not the duke, your father, an honest man? And your brother now foolishly takes after him, whose credulities, when I had already cozened, I was bound to appear stoical, to preserve the opinion they had conceived of me. I confess, and, were you in public, I would urge many empty names to fright you; put on my holiday countenance, and talk nothing but divinity, and golden sentences; look like a supercilious elder, with a starched face, and a tunable nose, whilst he is edifying his neighbor's woman. Do but fashion yourself to seem holy, and study to be worse in private, worse; you'll find yourself more active in your sensuality, and it will be another titillation, to think what an ass you make of the believing world, that will be ready to dote, nay, superstitiously adore you, for abusing them. How do you think a man should subsist? Wenching! Why, 'tis the top branch, the heart, the very soul of pleasure; I'll not give a chip to be an emperor an I may not curvet as often as my constitution requires. Lechery is the monarch of delight, whose throne is in the blood, to which all other sins do homage, and bow like serviceable vassals, petty subjects in the dominion of the flesh. Wenches! Why I have as many — yet, now I think better on it, I'll keep that to myself; store makes a good proverb. You little imagine (though I be married) that I am the greatest whoremaster in the dukedom. My nun at home knows nothing. Like a mole in the earth, I work deep, but invisible; I have my private houses, my granaries, my magazines, bully, as many concubines, as would, collected, furnish the great Turk's seraglio. You are a novice in the art of Venus, and will tell tales out of school, like your weak gallants of the first chin, that will brag what ladies they have brought to their obedience; that think it a mighty honor, to discourse how many forts they have beleaguered, how many they have taken by battery, how many by composition, and how many by stratagem; that will proclaim, how this madam kisses, how like ivy the t'other bona roba embraced them, and with what activity a third plays her amorous prize; a fine commendation for such whelps, is it not?

The Lady's Last Stake

Colley Cibber   *Act II, scene ii; Comic*

Lord George: I'll tell you, Madam — about two years ago, I happened to make a country visit to my Lady Conquest, her mother, and one day, at the table, I remember, I was particularly pleased with the entertainment, and upon enquiry, found that the bill of fare was under the direction of mademoiselle here. Now it happened at that time, I was my self in want of a housekeeper, upon which account I thought it would not be amiss, if I now and then paid her a little particular civility. To be short, I fairly told her, I had a great mind to have a plain good house-wife about me, and dropped some broad hints, that the place might be hers for the asking. Would you believe it, Madam, if I'm alive, the creature grew so vain upon it, so deplorably mistook my meaning, that she told me, her fortune depended upon her mother's will, and therefore she could receive no proposals of marriage without her consent. Now after that unfortunate blunder of hers, whether I ever gave my lady the least trouble about the business, I leave to the small remainder of her own conscience. Madam, if there's any faith in my senses, her only charms then were, and are still not in raising of passion, but paste. I own I did voraciously admire her prodigious knack of making cheesecakes, tarts, custards, and syllabubs. Whether I'm in love or no, I leave to your Ladyship . . . In the meantime, I believe, our surest comfort will be to think well of ourselves, and let it alone.

Love for Love

Jeremy: Now, Heaven of Mercy continue the tax upon paper; you don't mean to write a play? Sir, if you please to give me a small certificate of three lines — only to certify those whom it may concern; That the Bearer hereof, Jeremy Fetch by name, has for the space of seven years truly and faithfully served Valentine Legend, Esq., and that he is not now turn'd away for any Misdemeanor; but does voluntarily dismiss his Master from an future Authority over him — Sir, it's impossible. I may die with you, starve with you, or be damned with your works: But to live even Three days, the life of a play, I no more expect it, than to be Canonized for a Muse after my Decease. Is this the way to recover your father's favor? Why, Sir Sampson will be irreconcilable. If your younger brother should come from the sea, he'd never look upon you again. You're undone, Sir, you're ruined. You won't have a friend left in the world, if you turn poet. — Ah, pox confound that Will's Coffee-House, it has ruined more young men than the Royal Oak Lottery. Nothing thrives that belongs to't. The man of the house would have been an Alderman by this time with half the trade, if he had set up in the city. For my part, I never sit at the door, that I don't get double the stomach that I do at a horse race. The air upon Banstead Downs is nothing to it for a whetter; yet I never see it, but the spirit of famine appears to me, sometimes like a decayed Porter, worn out with pimping, and carrying Billets-doux, and Songs; not like other Porters for Hire, but for the Jest's sake. Now like a thin chairman, melted down to half his proportion, with carrying a Poet upon tick, to visit some great fortune; and his fare to be paid him like the wages of sin, either at the day of marriage, or the day of death. Sometimes like a bilked Bookseller, with a meager terrified countenance that looks as if he had written for himself, or were resolved to turn Author, and bring the rest of his Brethren into the same condition. And lastly, in the form of a worn-out Punk, with verses in her hand, which her vanity has preferred to settlements, without a whole tatter to her tail, but as ragged as one of the Muses; or if she were carrying her linen to the Paper-Mill, to be converted into Folio books, of warning to all young maids, not to prefer poetry to good sense, or lying in the arms of a needy wit, before the embraces of a wealthy fool.

Love Tricks

James Shirley   *Act III, scene i; Comic*

Rufaldo: 'Tis now early day; fie, what a long night hath this been! The sun went drunk to bed the last night, and could not see to rise this morning. I could hardly wink, I am sure, love kept me waking; and the expectation of this my wedding day did so caper in my brains, I thought of nothing but dancing the Shaking of the Sheets with my sweetheart. It is certain I am young, every body now tells me so, it did appear by Selina's consenting so soon to love; for when I had but broke the ice of my affection, she fell head over heels in love with me. Was ever man so happy as I am? I do feel, I do feel my years dropping off, as the rain from a man that comes dropping in. I do feel myself every day grow younger and younger still. Let me see, an hundred years hence, if I live to it, I shall be new out of my teens, and running into years of discretion again. Well, I will now to Master Cornelio's, and bid them good morrow with a noise of musicians; and to see, at the very talking of music, how my heart leaps and dances at my wedding already! I have bespoke the parson to marry us, and have promised him a double fee for expedition. Oh, now I am so proud of my joy, my feet do not know what ground they stand on.

The Minor

Smirk: We have an auction at twelve. Last week, amongst the valuable effects of a gentleman going abroad, I sold a choice collection of china, with a curious service of plate, though the real party was never master of above two delft dishes and a dozen of pewter, in all his life . . . Did you ever hear, Sir George what first brought me into the business? Quite an accident . . . You must have known my predecessor, Mr. Prig, the greatest man in the world, in his way, ay that ever was or ever will be; quite a jewel of a man; he would touch you up a lot; there was no resisting him. He would force you to bid, whether you would or no. I shall never see his equal. Far be it from me to vie with so great a man. But, as I was saying, my predecessor, Mr. Prig, was to have a sale, as it might be, on a Saturday. On Friday at noon (I shall never forget the day) he was suddenly seized with a violent colic. He sent for me to his bed-side, squeezed me by the hand, "Dear Smirk," said he, "what an accident! You know what is tomorrow: the greatest show this season; prints, pictures, bronzes, butterflies, medals and mignonettes; all the world will be there, Lady Dy Joss, Mrs. Nankyn, the Duchess of Dupe and everybody at all. You see my state, it will be impossible for me to mount. What can I do." It was not for me, you know, to advise that great man . . . At last, looking wistfully at me, "Smirk," says he, "do you love me?" "Mr Prig, can you doubt it?" "I'll put it to the test," says he. "Supply my place tomorrow." I, eager to show my love, rashly and rapidly replied, "I will." Absolute madness. But I had gone too far to recede. The point was, to prepare for the awful occasion. The first want that occurred to me was a wig. But this was too material an article to depend on my own judgment. I resolved to consult my friends. I told them the affair: "You hear, gentlemen, what has happened: Mr. Prig, one of the greatest men in his way the world ever saw, or ever will, quite a jewel of a man, take with a violent fit of colic; tomorrow, the greatest show this season: prints, pictures, bronzes, butterflies, medals and mignonettes; everybody in the world to be there; Lady Dy Joss, Mrs. Nankyn, Duchess of Dupe and all mankind; it being impossible he should mount, I have consented to sell —" They stared. "It is true, gentlemen. Now I should be glad to have your opinions as to a wig." They were divided; some recommended a tie, others a bag; one mentioned a bob, but was soon over-ruled. Now, for my part, I own, I rather inclined to the bag, but to avoid the imputation of rashness, I resolved to take Mrs. Smirk's judgment, my wife, a good, dear women, fine in figure, high in taste, a superior genius, and knows old china like a Nabob. I told her the case. "My dear, you know what has happened, Mr. Prig, the greatest man in the world, in his way, that ever was, or ever will be, quite a jewel of a man, a violent fit of colic — the greatest show this season tomorrow, pictures and everything in the world; all the world will be there. Now as it is impossible he should, I mount in his stead. You know the importance of a wig; I have asked my friends — some recommended a tie, some a bag — what is your opinion." "Why, to deal freely, Mr. Smirk," said she, "a tie for your round, regular, smiling face would be rather too formal, and a bag too boyish, deficient in dignity for the solemn occasion. Were I worthy to advise you, you should wear a something between both." "I'll be hanged if you don't mean a major." I jumped at the hint, and a major it was. But the next day, when I came to mount the rostrum, then was the trial. My limbs shook and my tongue trembled. The first lot was a chamber utensil, in Chelsea china, of the pea-green pattern. It occasioned a great laugh, but I got through it. Her grace, indeed, gave me great encouragement. I overheard her whisper to Lady Dy, "Upon my word, Mr. Smirk does it very well." "Very well indeed, Mr. Smirk," addressing herself to me. I made an acknowledging bow to her grace, as in duty bound. But, one flower flounced involuntarily from me that day, as I may say. I remember, Dr. Trifle called it enthusiastic, and pronounced it a presage of my future greatness. Why, sir, the lot was a Guido; a single figure, a marvelous fine performance, well preserved and highly finished. It stuck at five and forty. I charmed with the picture and piqued at the people. "A-going for five and forty, nobody more than five and forty — Pray, ladies and gentlemen, look at this piece, quite flesh and blood and only wants a touch from the torch of Prometheus to start from the canvas to fall a bidding." A general plaudit ensued, and in three minutes, knocked it down at sixty-three ten. The great nicety of our art is the eye. Mark how mine skims around the room. Some bidders are shy, and only advance with a nod; but I nail them. One, two, three, four, five. You will be surprised!

The Mistake

Sir John Vanbrugh   *Act V; Comic*

Lopez: As soon as it is night, says my master to me, though it
cost me my life, I'll enter Leonora's lodgings; therefore make
haste, Lopez, prepare everything necessary, three pair of pock-
et-pistols, two wide mouthed blunderbusses, some six ells of
sword blade, and a couple of dark lanterns. When my master
said this to me; Sir, said I to my master, (that it, I would have
said it if I had not been in such a fright I could say nothing;
however, I'll say it to him now, and shall probably have a
quiet hearing) look you, sir, by dint of reason I intend to confound you. You are resolved, you say, to get into Leonora's
lodgings, though the devil stand in the doorway? — Yes,
Lopez, that's my resolution. — Very well; and what do you
intend to do when you are there? — Why, what an injured
man should do; make her sensible of — Make her sensible of
a pudding! don't you see she's a jade? She'll raise the house
about your ears, arm the whole family, set the great dog at
you. — Were there legions of devils to repulse me, in such a
cause I sir, you may leave me at home to lay the cloth. — No;
thou art my ancient friend, my fellow traveler, and to reward
thy faithful services, this night thou shalt partake my danger
and my glory. — Sir, I have got glory enough under you
already, to content any reasonable servant for life. — Thy
modesty makes me willing to double my bounty; this night
may bring eternal honor to thee and thy family. — Eternal
honor, sir, is too much in conscience for a serving-man;
besides, ambition has been many a great soul's undoing. — I
doubt thou art afraid, my Lopez; thou shalt be armed with
back, with breast, and headpiece. — They will encumber me
in my retreat. — Retreat, my hero! thou never shalt retreat.
— Then by my troth, I'll never go, sir!

The Old Bachelor

William Congreve   *Act III, scene ii; Comic*

Heartwell: Well, has this prevailed for me, and will you look upon me? Why, 'twas I sung and danced; I gave music to the voice, and life to their measures. Look you here, Sylvia, here are songs and dances, poetry and music — hark! [pulling out a purse and chinking it] how sweetly one guinea rhymes to another, and how they dance to the music of their own chink. This buys all the 'tother — and this thou shalt have; and all that I am worth for the purchase of thy love. Say, is it mine then, ha? Speak, Siren. — Oons, why do I look on her! Yet I must. Speak, dear angel, devil, saint, witch, do not rack me in suspense. Oh, manhood, where art thou! What am I come to? A woman's toy at these years! Death, a bearded baby for a girl to dandle. Oh, dotage, dotage! That ever that noble passion, lust, should ebb to this degree. No reflux of vigorous blood, but milky love supplies the empty channels and prompts me to the softness of a child, a mere infant, and would suck. Can you love me, Sylvia? Speak. Pox, how her innocence torments and pleases me! Lying, child, is indeed the art of love, and men are generally masters in it. But I'm so newly entered, you cannot distrust me of any skill in the treacherous mystery. Now by my soul, I cannot lie, though it were to serve a friend, or gain a mistress. No, no, dear ignorance, thou beauteous Changeling, I tell thee I do love thee, and tell it for a truth, a naked truth, which I'm ashamed to discover. And a pox upon me for loving thee so well! Yet I must on — 'tis a bearded arrow, and will more easily be thrust forward than drawn back. But how can you be well assured? Take the symptoms and ask all the tyrants of thy sex, if their fools are not known by this parti-colored livery. I am melancholy when thou art absent; look like an ass when you art present, wake for you when I should sleep, and even dream of you when I am awake; sigh much, drink little, eat less, court solitude, am grown very entertaining to myself and (as I am informed) very troublesome to everybody else. If this be not love, it is madness, and then it is pardonable — Nay yet a more certain sign than all this — I give thee my money.

The Old Bachelor

William Congreve   *Act IV, scene i; Comic*

Fondlewife: Go in and bid my Cocky come out to me. I will
give her some instructions; I will reason with her before I go.
And in the meantime, I will reason with myself — Tell me,
Isaac, why art thee jealous? Why art thee distrustful of the
wife of thy bosom? Because she is young and vigorous, and I
am old and impotent. Then why didst thee marry, Isaac?
Because she was beautiful and tempting, and because I was
obstinate and doting, so that my inclination was (and is still)
greater than my power. — And will not that which tempted
thee, also tempt others, who will tempt her, Isaac? — I fear it
much. — But does not thy wife love thee, nay, dote upon
thee? — Yes! — Why then — Ay, but to say truth, she's
fonder of me than she has reason to be, and in the way of
trade we still suspect the smoothest dealers of the deepest
designs. — And that she has some design deeper than thou
canst reach, th' hast experimented, Isaac. — But mum. Wife
— have you throughly considered how detestable, how
heinous, and how crying a sin the sin of adultery is? Have
you weighed it, I say? For it is a very weighty sin, and
although it may lie heavy upon thee, yet thy husband must
also bear his part: for thy iniquity will fall upon his head.
[aside] I profess, she has an alluring eye; I am doubtful
whether I shall trust her even with Tribulation himself —
Speak, I say. Have you considered what it is to cuckold your
husband? [aside] Verily, I fear I have carried the jest too far.
Nay look you now if she does not weep — 'Tis the fondest
fool. — Nay, Cocky, Cocky, nay, dear Cocky, don't cry. I was
but in jest, I was not ifeck. Good lack, good lack, she would
melt a heart of oak — I profess, I can hold no longer. Nay,
dear Cocky — Ifeck, you'll break my heart — Ifeck you will.
See, you have made me weep — made poor Nykin weep.

Nay, come kiss, buss poor Nykin, and I won't leave thee —
I'll lose all first. Won't you kiss Nykin? What, not love
Cocky? I profess I do love thee better than 500 pound — and
so thou shalt say, for I'll leave it to stay with thee. Poor
Cocky, Kiss Nykin, kiss Nykin, ee,ee,ee. Here will be the
good man anon, to talk to Cocky, and teach her how a wife
ought to behave herself. That's my good dear. Come, kiss
Nykin once more, and then get you in — so. Get you in, get
you in —so. Get you in, get you in. Bye,bye. Bye, Cocky, bye
Cocky. Bye bye.

The Projectors

John Wilson   *Act II, scene i; Comic*

Leanchops: Well! 'o my conscience, there was never so unlucky a
fellow as myself! Here I live with a master that has wealth
enough; but so fearful, sad, pensive, suspicious a fellow, that
he disquiets both himself and everyone else! Art, I have heard
say, has but seven liberal sciences, but he has a thousand illib-
eral! There lives not a more base, niggardly, unsatiable, pinch-
penny, nor a more gaping, griping, polling, extorting
devouring cormorant! A sponge sucks not up faster, and yet a
pumice gives back easier! He shall watch you a young heir as
diligently as a raven a dying horse, and yet swallow him with
more tears than a crocodile! He never sleeps but he seals up
the nose of his bellows, lest they lose breath, and has almost
broke his brains to find the like device for his chimney and
his throat! A gamester has not studied the advantage of dice
half so much as he a sordid parsimony, which yet he calls
thrift; and will tell you to a crumb how much difference there
is in point of loss between a hundred dozen of bread broken
with the hand and cut with a knife. The devil's in him, and I
am as weary of him as of our last journey, which both of us
perform'd on the same horse! As thus: — In the morning,
about two hours before him, out gets Peel Garlick, he jogs
after, overtakes me, rides through the next town and a little
beyond it, leaving his palfrey agrazing for me and marches on
himself. In like manner I get up, overtake him, ride on, and
leave him on this side the next town, and so order our business, that he rides out in the morning and into the inn at
night, and through every town by the way. Nor need we fear
any man's stealing him! Smithfield, at the end of a long vaca-
tion, can't show such another wall-ey'd, crestfallen, saddle-
back'd, flat-ribb'd, gut-founder'd, shoulder-pitch'd, spur-gall'd,
hip-shotten, grease-moulten jade, besides splint, spavin, glan-
ders, farce, stringhalt, sprains, scratches, malander and wind-

galls innumerable! Like the fool's hobby-horse, were it not for the name of a horse a man had as lief go afoot, and thus we jog on in grief together.

The Projectors

John Wilson   *Act II, scene i; Comic*

Suckdry: So! He's gone! And I'll go visit my gold! I am afraid I have spoken in my sleep, or dropped some word or other that may discover it, or that this rogue has eyes in his poll, and observ'd where I buried it. But if he has, I'll so dig 'um out! I have reason enough to suspect it — men speak more heartily to me than they were wont, are more free in their salutes, stop and talk with me, shake me by the hand, ask me how I do, whither I am going, what's my business, if they may serve me, and the like! Nay, Mr. Jocose t'other day would have given me wine, and proffered his son should marry my daughter — without a portion, too! Ah-ha! I do not like when rich men speak kindly to a poor man; they offer bread with one hand, but carry a stone in t'other! But I lose time! My gold, my gold! This must be the place! All's safe, and I'm alive again! All hail, thou that givest form to everything! Thou sun of life! Thou guardian that protectest us! Thou regent of the world, that disposeth of all things as thou best pleaseth, and without whom human society would quickly fall in pieces! For, whatever else may be called the girdle, I am sure thou art the buckle that hold'st it together! There! Rest in peace, my better angels! And while I call ye mine, let the world frown, laugh, point, or hiss — one glance of yours is worth it all; and I shall want nothing but too few arms to hug myself! I shall be courted by every man, welcome everywhere — at least from the teeth outwards; for in this world gold seasons and relishes everything, and men are received, not for the ass's, but for the goddess's sake! 'Tis like having a handsome wife — every man is, or would be, your servant!

Sir Courtly Nice

John Crowne   *Act II, scene i; Comic*

Farewel: Oh! Fire and water are not so contrary. Sir Courtly is so civil a creature, and so respectful to everything belongs to a gentleman, he stands bare to his own periwig. Surly uncovers to nothing but his own nightcap, nor to that if he be drunk, for he sleeps in his hat. Sir Courtly is so gentle a creature, he writes a challenge in the style of a billet-doux. Surly talks to his mistress as he would to a hector that wins his money. Sir Courtly is so pleased with his own person, his daily contemplation, nay, his salvation is a looking glass, for there he finds eternal happiness. Surly's heaven, at least his priest, is his claret glass; for to that he confesses all his sins, and receives from it absolution and comfort. But his damnation is a looking glass, for there he finds an eternal fire in his nose. In short, if you would make a posset for the devil, mingle these two, for there never was so sweet a thing as Sir Court, so sour as Surly.

The Soldier's Fortune

Thomas Otway   *Act II; Comic*

Sir David: Well, of all blessings, a discreet wife is the greatest
  that can light upon a man of years: had I been married to any
  thing but an angel now, what a beast I had been by this time!
  Well, I am the happiest old fool! 'Tis an horrid age that we
  live in, so than an honest man can keep nothing to himself; if
  you have a good estate, every covetous rogue is longing for't
  (truly I love a good estate dearly myself), if you have a handsome wife, every smooth faced coxcomb will be combing and
  cocking at her, flesh-flies are not so troublesome to the sham-
  bles as those sort of insects are to the boxes in the play-house.
  But virtue is a great blessing, an unvaluable treasure; to tell
  me her self that a villain had tempted her, and give me the
  very picture, the enchantment he sent to bewitch her, it
  strikes me dumb with admiration; here's the villain in effigy.
  [Pulls out the picture]. Odd a very handsome fellow, a dangerous rogue, I'll warrant him, such fellows as these now
  should be fettered like unruly colts, that they might not leap
  into other men's pastures. Here's a nose now I could find it in
  my heart to cut it off; damned dog, to dare to presume to
  make a cuckold of a knight! Bless us, what will this world
  come to? Well, poor Sir David, down, down on thy knees,
  and thank thy stars for this deliverance.

The Virtuoso

Thomas Shadwell   *Act III, scene iv; Comic*

Sir Formal: Gentlemen and ladies, some affairs have engaged my noble friend Sir Nicholas to borrow himself of you a while, and he has commanded me to pawn my person till he shall redeem it with his own. Whatever is within the sphere of my activity, you must command. I must confess I have some felicity in speaking. We orators speak alike upon all subjects. My speeches are all so subtly designed that whatever I speak in praise of anything with very little alteration will serve in praise of the contrary. 'Tis all one to me. I am ready to speak upon all occasions. Now I am inspired with eloquence. Hem. Hem. Being one day, most noble auditors, musing in my study upon the too fleeting condition of poor humankind, I observed, not far from the scene of my meditation, an excellent machine called a mousetrap (which my man had placed there) which had included in it a solitary mouse, which pensive prisoner, in vain bewailing its own misfortunes and the precipitation of its too unadvised attempt, still struggling for liberty against the too stubborn opposition of solid wood and more obdurate wire, at last, the pretty malefactor having tired, alas, its too feeble limbs till they became languid in fruitless endeavors for its excarceration, the pretty felon — since it could not break its prison, and, its offense being beyond the benefit of clergy, could hope for no bail — at last sat still, pensively lamenting the severity of its fate and the narrowness of its, alas, too withering durance. After I had contemplated a while upon the no little curiosity of the engine and the subtlety of its inventor, I began to reflect upon the enticement which so fatally betrayed the uncautious animal to its sudden ruin; and found it to be the too, alas, specious bait of Cheshire cheese, which seems to be a great delicate to the palate of this animal who, in seeking to preserve its life, oh, misfortune, took the certain means to death, and searching for its livelihood had sadly encountered its own destruction.

The Way of the World

William Congreve   *Act IV, scene i; Comic*

Mirabell: Well, have I liberty to offer Conditions — that when
you are dwindl'd into a Wife, I may not be beyond Measure
enlarg'd into a Husband? Imprimis, then, I Covenant that
your acquaintance shall be General, that you admit no sworn
Confidant, or Intimate of your own Sex; no She friend to
screen her affairs under your countenance and tempt you to
make trial of a Mutual Secrecy. No decoy duck to wheadle
you a fop —- scrambling to the play in a Mask — then bring
you home in a pretended fright, when you think you shall be
found out. — And rail at me for missing the play, and disap-
pointing the frolic which you had to pick me up and prove
my Constancy . . . Item, I Article that you continue to like
your own face as long as I shall. And while it passes current
with me, that you endeavor not to new Coin it. To which
end, together, with all Vizards for the day, I prohibit all
Masks for the night. made of oil'd skins and I know not what
— Hog's bones, hare's gall, Pig-water, and the marrow of a
roasted cat. In short, I forbid all Commerce with the
Gentlewomen in what-de-call-it Court. Item, I shut my
doors against all bawds with baskets and penny-worths of
Muslin, China, Fans, Atlases, etc. Item, when you shall be
breeding . . . Which may be presum'd with a blessing on our
endeavors . . . I denounce against all strait-lacing, Squeezing
for a Shape, till you mold my boy's head like a sugar-loaf; and
instead of a man-child, make me the Father to a Crooked-bil-
let. Lastly, to the dominion of the Tea-Table, I submit. —
But with proviso that you exceed not in your province; but
restrain yourself to nature and simple Tea-Table drinks, as
Tea, Chocolate, and Coffee. As likewise to Genuine, and
Authoriz'd, Tea-Table talk — such as mending of Fashions,
spoiling reputations, railing at absent friends, and so forth —

but that on no account you encroach upon the men's prerogative, and presume to drink healths, or toast fellows; for prevention of which, I banish all Foreign Forces, all Auxiliaries to the Tea-Table, as Orange-Brandy, all Anniseed, Cinnamon, Citron, and Barbados Waters, together with Ratafia, and the most noble spirit of Clary, — but for Cowslip-Wine, Poppy-Water, and all Dormitives, those I allow.— These provisos admitted, in other things I may prove a tractable and complying husband.

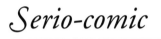

Serio-comic

All Mistaken, or, The Mad Couple

Philidor: I have been quite at t'other end o'th' town,
   To put my children out to new nurses,
   For I am known to every nurse hereabout;
   That they will as soon nurse a cat's kitten
   As any child of mine. This is a very
   Pleasant life I lead, neither is this the
   Worst part of it; for there are a certain
   Flock of women that I have promis'd marriage,
   I expect a volley of shot from them too,
   Soon as they find me out. Would wives and children
   Were as hard to come by as money, then would
   I turn usurer, and let 'em out to use;
   For, to say truth, I have enough to spare.
   So, here comes one of my promis'd Virgins!
   Nay, a second, too — a third — a fourth — a fifth —
   A sixth — Welcome, blessed half dozen; now will I go
   Muster my nurses and children, too, and go
   Against the Great Turk. I am glad to see
   They have brought ne'er a coffin, for I expect
   Nothing but death from them. I wonder they don't
   Begin to ring my funeral peal. See every
   One of them beckons to me, as much as to say,
   I'd speak with you in private; but the devil
   Take me if e'er a one of them do; I find
   By this they would not have their business known
   To one another; this may be a means for me
   To get off for this time — Ladies, you all
   Look as if you had something to say to
   Me; pray, make me so happy as to let
   Me know what 'tis. [Aside] They dare not speak aloud.
   Will you, Madam? or you? or you, madam? Or you,

Madam? What, not one of you tell me what
The honor of these visits mean? I see
I am troublesome to you all, therefore
I'll not be longer rude; and so I take
My leave. — This was good luck, that they should come
All together; for I had rather be
Alone six hours with the devil, than with
E'er a one of them an half hour — I'll stand close
In this corner till they are all gone.

The Cheats

John Wilson   *Act I, scene ii; Serio-Comic*

Jolly: If you must love, love on; but go no further.
   Women enjoy'd like rivers in the sea,
   Lose both their taste and name. Suppose 'em Junoes
   In the pursuit, they're clouds in the enjoyment.
   Suppose her handsome, she's a honey-pot
   I'th'sun; if otherwise, you'll ne'er endure her:
   If honest, insolent, though ne'er so ugly:
   She thinks you are beholden to her for't;
   And yet, who knows how long she may be so.
   Is she the map of modesty? Perhaps
   'Tis but your own opinion; love is blind.
   There's many pass for such, whose husbands yet
   Could, if they durst, tell you another tale.
   Is she a housewife? Can she make a band?
   Order a dairy? Cure a broken shin?
   Examine your accounts, and at year's end
   Pray tell me what you've saved. Is she highborn?
   Twenty to one she's proud, and quickly scorns you.
   What are you better for those doughty acts
   My lord her great-great-grandfather perform'd
   The Lord knows where? or 'thave her portion paid you
   In genealogies, gilt spurs, and cantons? Consider,
   'Tis like a battle, to be fought but once;
   And therefore, it must be so, be sure
   She be your equal, and if possible virtuous —
   At least not tainted with her mother's vices.
   And now, if after this thou dar'st be wiving,
   Th'art a bold fellow; and that's all I'll say.

The Cheats

John Wilson   *Act IV, scene ii; Serio-Comic*

Mopus: You are gentlemen, and, I see, understand. I'll be plain
with you. Examine the world, and you'll find three-quarters
of it downright fools, and for the rest, six parts in seven little
besides band and beard, and yet they make a great bustle in
the world, and pass for shrewd men! And can you blame me,
then? Did you ever hear a fishwife cry, "Stinking mackerel"?
Or a citizen, "Gummed velvet"? No! The best in the town,
though the worst in his shop! Here we have a learned consul-
tation, whether my lady may eat butter with her eggs, or have
her posset turn'd with lemon or ale. Yonder another keeps a
sputter, with his new! new! new! The wall-eyed mare, and the
cropt flea-bitten; a book with a hard title; a new found language in Ireland; Turk and Pope; the flesh office; my lady's
dog; the safest way of cutting of corns; a bag of writings; a
house of the Bank-side, the christening of another Turk; a
Franciscan proselyte, gentlemen-ushers, and maid servants;
dentifrices and lozenges. Another daubs you whole volumes
with the difference between sufficient and efficacious.
Another, whether the lining of Aaron's ephod were sky col-
ored or sea green; and hack and hew so desperately about
their goats' wool, a man would bless himself to see such piles
of elaborate nonsense! And now, gentlemen, am I the only
man in fault? The worst you can say is, the people have so little wit as to give me money; and I am so mad as to pocket the
injury! Does this satisfy?

The Choleric Fathers (A Comic Opera)

Thomas Holcroft   *Serio-Comic*

Don Julio Pimiento: Really, my dear, you understand Hocus
Pocus very well; but pray move a little farther that way — a
little farther [Finds letter in bag] Ha, child! Yes, they are here
I believe — My friend the Philosopher was very right —
Love letters here are — Rope ladders, and elopements will
come next, I suppose — But we shall see — [Takes the
Letters out] How! What! 'To the most famous, most famous,
most renowned Master of all Science, Dr. Don Lilibulero'.
Indeed! 'Dearest Zelida' — begins very learnedly! — ''Tis
impossible to express the torments I this moment suffer — I
have sent you his by my Valet, disguised purposely to deceive
your father; hope you will lend him you assistance' —- Ah,
that he need not doubt of — 'Consider, Zelida, my life is at
stake! to outwit those who would sacrifice our happiness to
their own caprice will be meritorious; we cannot better fulfill
our duty' — Most dutiful, Sir — 'Life or death will be the
consequence of your answer, to the hoping, despairing, miserable,
    FERNANDO'
And miserable may you remains! — So, Madam! — So Mr.
Philosopher! These are your secrets — And — [To Jaquelina]
you! Mrs. Ten Ducats! — But he is gone to prepare the second part, I shall be sure to see him again — So, most dutiful
Lady! You, who are a pattern of virtue, and discretion, and
meekness. You can give countenance to impostors and join in
rendering your father ridiculous to the whole work — But
this, no doubt, is your answer. 'To Don Fernando.' Yes, yes
— we shall not see your dutiful sentiments displayed at full
length; I shall find here myself painted in most beautiful col-
ors . . . Indiscretion! A most gentle term indeed for conspir-
ing to dishonor your family, to disgrace your father, and to

render him the subject of a footman's ballad in every twopenny taphouse — But we shall see, we shall see [Opens the letter and reads] 'I am ashamed of myself' — Well you may, indeed! — 'I am ashamed of myself when I find my conduct has been such, Fernando, as could authorize your present proceedings' — how, how! — 'I must be the most undutiful, the worst of children, could I, any way, willfully contribute to see my father so indecently imposed upon" — [Looks at Zelida] — My girl! my child! — 'When authorized by my father, I did not scruple to confess my affection for you, nor do I, still, to own that his consent to our union would, perhaps, give me as much pleasure as you; but without his consent, I never will be yours,' — Zelida! — 'I cannot pardon myself for having received your letter without his knowledge; and I assure you, no power on earth shall ever make me yours, if, after the receipt of this, you continue to impose on him by means which, though perhaps not so considered by you, are degrading and insulting.' [Don Pimiento weeps aloud and lets the letter fall out of his hands] Zelida! — You are a good girl, Zelida! A good girl! — But that damned rascal, that Philosopher, that footman, that scoundrel . . . I'll be revenged! Damn philosophy! I'll be revenged!

The City Nightcap

Robert Davenport   *Act II; Serio-Comic*

Philippo: Hear me, great sir; I will confess, Lorenzo,
And print thee down the fool of passion.
'Tis true, this boasting man did thus erect me
In his opinion, placed me in his love,
Grac'd me with courtesies: O, the craft of jealousy!
As boys, to take the bird, about the pit
Cast wheat and chaff, contriving a neat train
To entice her to her ruin — so this friend,
Falser than city oaths, it is not doubted,
Having so far endear'd me, when he came
To enjoy a fair wife, guess'd it impossible
For me to share with him in all things else
And not in her; for fair wives oft, we see,
Strike the discord in sweet friendship's harmony:
And having no way to ensnare me so,
To separate our loves, he seriously
Woo'd me to try his wife.
'Tis true,
By all that honest men may be believed by.
Three several times I tried her, by him urg'd to't.
Yet still my truth not started, kept so constant,
That till this hour this lady thus much knew not.
I bore her brave reproofs. O, when she spake,
The saints, sure, listened, and at every point
She got the applause of angels! Now, upon this,
This jealous lord infers (and it may be
But to shun futurity) that I,
His betray'd friend, could not hold the cup,
But I must drink the poison. No, Lorenzo,
An honest man is still an unmov'd rock,
Wash'd whiter, but not shaken with the shock.

Whose heart conceives no sinister device,
Fearless he plays with flames, and treads on ice.

The Clandestine Marriage

David Garrick & George Colman the Elder

Act I, scene i; Serio-Comic

Lovewell: My love! How's this? In tears? Indeed, this is too much. You promised me to support your spirits, and to wait the determination of our fortune with patience. For my sake, for your own, be comforted. Why will you study to add to our uneasiness and perplexity? Indeed, indeed, you are to blame. The amiable delicacy of your temper, and your quick sensibility, only serve to make you unhappy. To clear up this affair properly to Mr. Sterling is the continual employment of my thoughts. Everything now is in a fair train. It begins to grow ripe for a discovery; and I have no doubt of its concluding to the satisfaction of ourselves, of your father, and the whole family. You put me upon the rack. I would do anything to make you easy. But you know your father's temper. Money (you will excuse my frankness) is the spring of all his actions, which nothing but the idea of acquiring nobility or magnificence can ever make him forego — and these he thinks his money will purchase. You know, too, your aunt, Mrs. Heidelberg's, notions of the splendor of high life, her contempt for everything that does not relish of what she calls Quality, and that from the vast fortune in her hands, by her late husband, she absolutely governs Mr. Sterling and the whole family. Now if they should come to the knowledge of this affair too abruptly, they might, perhaps, be incensed beyond all hopes of reconciliation. I meant to discover it soon, but would not do it too precipitately. I have more than once sounded Mr. Sterling about it, and will attempt him more seriously the next opportunity. But my principal hopes are these. My relationship to Lord Ogleby, and his having placed me with your father, have been, you know, the first links in the chain of this connection between the two families, In consequence of which, I am at present in high favor with all parties. While they all remain thus well affected to me, I propose to lay our case before the old lord; and if I can prevail on him to mediate in this affair, I make no doubt but he will be able to appease your father; and being a lord and a man of quality, I am sure he may bring Mrs. Heidelberg into good humor at any time. Let me beg you, therefore, to have but a little patience, as, you see, we are upon the very eve of a discovery that must probably be to our advantage. But in the meantime, make yourself easy.

fe: What, writing more letters? How's this? Nay, you ..ot stir, Madam. "Dear, dear, dear, Mr. Horner" — very .. — I have taught you to write letters to good purpose — .ut let's see it. "First I am to beg your pardon for my boldness in writing to you, which I'd have you to know, I would not have done, had not you said first you loved me so extremely, which, if you do, you will never suffer me to lie in the arms of another man, whom I loath, nauseate, and detest" — Now you can write these filthy words, but what follows — "Therefore I hope you will speedily find some way to free me from this unfortunate match, which was never, I assure you, of my choice, but I'm afraid 'tis already gone too far; however, if you love me, as I do you, you will try what you can do, but you must help me away before tomorrow, or else, alas, I shall be for ever out of your reach, for I can defer no longer our — our" — [The letter concludes]. What is to follow "our"? Speak, what? Our journey into the country, I suppose. Oh, woman, damned woman, and love, damned love, their old tempter, for this is one of his miracles: in a moment, he can make those blind that could see, and those see that were blind, those dumb that could speak, and those prattle who were dumb before, nay what is more than all, make those dough baked, senseless, indocile animals, women, too hard for us their politic lords and rulers in a moment; but make an end of your letter, and then I'll make an end of you thus, and all my plagues together.

The Double Dealer

William Congreve   *Act II, scene i; Serio-Comic*

Maskwell: Till then Success will attend me; for when I meet
you, I meet the only Obstacle to my Fortune. Cynthia, let
thy Beauty gild my Crimes; and whatsoever I commit of
Treachery or Deceit shall be imputed to me as a Merit. —
Treachery? What Treachery? Love cancels all Bonds of
Friendship, and sets men right upon their first foundations.

Duty to Kings, Piety to Parents, Gratitude to Benefactors,
and Fidelity to Friends, are different and particular ties: but
the Name of Rival cuts 'em all asunder and is a general
acquittance. Rival is equal, and Love like Death a universal
Leveller of Mankind. Ha! But is there not such a thing as
Honesty? Yes, and whosoever has it about him, bears an
Enemy in his Breast. For your honest man, as I take it, is that
nice, scrupulous, conscientious Person, who will cheat no
body but himself; such another Coxcomb as your wise man,
who is too hard for all the World, and will be made a Fool of
by nobody but himself; Ha,ha, ha. Well, for Wisdom and
Honesty, give me Cunning and Hypocrisy; Oh, 'tis such a
pleasure to angle for fair-faced Fools! Then that hungry
gullible Credulity will bite at anything. — Why, let me see, I
have the same Face, the same Words and Accents when I
speak what I do think, and when I speak what I do not think
— the very same — and dear dissimulation is the only Art
not to be known from Nature.
Why will Mankind be Fools, and be deceiv'd?
And why are Friends and Lovers' Oaths believ'd,
When each, who searched strictly his own mind,
May so much Fraud and Power of Baseness find?

The Dutch Courtesan

John Marston   Act I, scene i; Serio-C

Freevill: Alas, good creatures, what would you have them
Would you have them get their living by the curse of n
the sweat of their brows? So they do. Every man must foll
his trade, and every woman her occupation. A poor, decaye
mechanical's wife, her husband is laid up; may she not lawful-
ly be laid down when her husband's only rising is by his wife's
falling? A captain's wife wants means, her commander lies in
open field abroad; may not she lie in civil arms at home? A
waiting gentlewoman, that had wont to take say to her lady,
miscarries or so; the court misfortune throws her down; may
not the city courtesy take her up? Do you know no alderman
would pity such a woman's case? Why is charity grown a sin?
or relieving the poor and impotent an offense? You will say
beasts take no money for their fleshly entertainment. True,
because they are beasts, therefore beastly; only men give to
loose because they are men, therefore manly; and indeed,
wherein should they bestow their money better? In land, the
title may be crack'd; in houses, they may be burnt; in apparel,
'twill wear; in wine, alas, for pity, our throat is but short. But
employ your money upon women, and, a thousand to nothing, some one of them will bestow that on you which shall
stick by you as long as you live. They are no ingrateful persons; they will give quid for quo: do ye protest, they'll swear;
do you rise, they'll fall; do you fall, they'll rise; do you give
them the French crown, they'll give you the French — O jus-
tus justa justum! They sell their bodies; do not better persons
sell their souls? Nay, since all things have been sold — honor,
justice, faith, nay, even God himself —
Ay me, what base ignobleness is it
To sell the pleasure of a wanton bed?
Why do men scrape, why heap to full heaps join?

But for his mistress, who would care for coin?
For this I hold to be denied of no man:
All things are made for man, and man for woman.
Give me my fee!

The Lady's Last Stake

Colley Cibber   *Act I, scene i; Serio-Comic*

Lord Wronglove: My wife, as abundance of other men of quality's wives are, is a miserable woman. Ask her the reason, she'll tell you — Husband, ask me. I say, Wife — all's entirely owing to her own temper. This continual jealousy is insupportable. What's to be done with her? What's her complaint? Who's the aggressor? I even refer the matter fairly to my own conscience, and if she casts me there, I'll do her justice; if not, though the cost were ten times hers, I'll make my self easy, for the rest of my life. Let me see — as to the fact that I'm charged with, viz., That I have feloniously embezzled my inclinations among the rough and smooth conversation of several undaunted gentlewomen, and so forth — That, I think, since it must be proved against me, I had best plead guilty to. Be it so. Very well! A terrible charge indeed. And now, now let's hear the defendant, and then proceed to judgment and damages. Well! the defendant says, That 'tis true he was in love with madam up to her proud heart's wishes, but hoped that marriage was his end of servitude, that then her wifely reserve, her pride, and other fine lady's airs would be all laid aside. No. Her ladyship was still the same unconquered heroine. If being endured could give me happiness, 'twas mine. If not, she knew herself, and should not bend below her sex's value. I bore this long, then urged her duty; that this reserve of humor was inconsistent with her being a friend, a wife, or a companion. She said 'twas nature's fault, and I but talked in vain. Upon this, I found my patience began to have enough on't, so I even made her invincibleship a low bow, and told her, I would dispose of my time in pleasures, which were a little more come at-able; which pleasures I have found, and she has found out, but truly she won't bear it. And though she scorned to love, she'll condescend to hate.

She'll have redress, revenge, and reparation, so that if I have a mind to be easy at home, I need but tremble at her anger, down on my knees, confess, beg pardon, promise amendment, keep my word, and the business is done. — Now, venerable human conscience, speak, must I do this only to purchase what the greatness of her soul has taught me to be indifferent to? Am I bound to fast, because her ladyship has no appetite? Shall threats and brow-beatings fright me into justice, where my own will's a law? — No, no, no, positively, no. I'm lord of my own heart, sure, and whoever thinks to enter at my humor shall speak me very fair. — Most generous conscience, I give you thanks for my deliverance! And since I'm positive I've little Nature on my side, too, Madam may now go on with her noble resentment as she pleases.

The Obstinate Lady

Sir Aston Cokain   *Act IV, scene ii; Serio-Comic*

Falorus: What ails me? Let me see —
What is the cause of such an alteration
I find within me? Doubtless it is love.
To whom? To whom but to the worthiest
And sweet Lucora? Take heed, 'tis dangerous!
A sudden ruin so will seize my friendship,
And prove my former protestations
Feign'd untruths. Cannot the noble name
Of young Carionil prevent me? No,
Nor certainty of all the evil wills
Of all the friends I have.
Were both our better genius orators,
And here embraced fast my knees and wept
Miraculous tears to quench the rising flames
Lucora's irresistible eyes have kindled
In me, or to drown this late impression love
Hath sealed upon my heart, I'd be as remorseless
As the most stern and unmoved Scythian,
And deafer than the people that inhabit
Near the Egyptian cataracts of the Nile.
But I am base, base to infringe the knot
Of amity a long and serious knowledge
Of each other hath tied betwixt us. 'Twere safer
Sailing with drunken mariners between
Hard Scylla and Charybdis, than to suffer
My much divided thought, and forth of them
To work such a conclusion to my passions
As might hereafter confirm me noble in
The opinion of the world. But I'm most ignorant,
And know not what to do. Would I were so
Distraught that my own self I could not know!

The Old Couple

Thomas May   *Act I; Serio-Comic*

Euphues: Rich Earthworm's son! Why, in the name of wonder
   Should it be her desire to speak with him?
   She knows him not. Well, let it be a riddle;
   I have not so much wit as to expound it;
   Nor yet so little as to lose my thoughts
   Or study to find out what the no reason
   Of a young wench's will is. Should I guess —
   I know not what to think; she may have heard
   That he's a proper man, and so desire
   To satisfy herself. What reason then
   Can she allege to him? Tut, that's not it:
   Her beauty and large dow'r need not to seek
   Out any suitors; and the odious name
   Of his old wretched father would quite choke it.
   Or have some tattling gossips or the maids
   Told her, perchance, that he's a conjuror?
   He goes in black; they say he is a scholar:
   Has been beyond the sea, too; there it may lie:
   And he must satisfy her longing thought,
   What or how many husbands she shall have;
   Of what degree, upon what night she shall
   Dream of the man; when she shall fast, and walk
   In the churchyard, to see him passing by
   Just in those clothes that first he comes a suitor.
   These things may be; but why should she make me
   To be her instrument? Some of the men
   Or maids might do't as well. Well, since you have
   Used me, fair cousin, I will sounds your drifts,
   Or't shall go hard. The fellow may abuse her;
   Therefore, I'll watch him, too, and straight about it.
   But now I think on't, I'll solicit him
   By letter first, and meet him afterward.

The Provoked Husband

Sir John Vanbrugh and Colley Cibber

Act I, scene i; Serio-Comic

Lord Townley: Why did I marry? Was it not evident my plain, rational scheme of life was impracticable, with a woman of so different a way of thinking? Is there one article of it that she has not broke in upon? Yet, let me do her justice — her reputation; that I have no reason to believe is in question. But then, how long her profligate course of pleasures may make her able to keep it — is a shocking question! And her presumption while she keeps it — insupportable! For on the pride of that single virtue she seems to lay it down, as a fundamental point, that the free indulgence of every other vice this fertile town affords is the birthright prerogative of a women of quality. Amazing that a creature so warm in the pursuit of her pleasures should never cast one thought towards her happiness. This, while she admits no lover, she thinks it a greater merit still, in her chastity, not to care for her husband; and while she herself is solacing in one continual round of cards and good company, he, poor wretch, is left at large to take care of his own contentment. 'Tis time, indeed, some care were taken, and speedily there shall be. Yet let me not be rash. Perhaps this disappointment of my heart may make me too impatient; and some tempers, when reproached, grow more untractable.

The Traitor

James Shirley   *Act II, scene i; Serio-Comic*

Sciarrha: What do great ladies do at court, I pray?
   Enjoy the pleasures of the world, dance, kiss
   The amorous lords, and change court breath, sing loose
   Belief of other heaven, tell wanton dreams,
   Rehearse your sprightly bed scenes, and boast which
   Hath most idolators, accuse all faces
   That trust to the simplicity of nature,
   Talk witty blasphemy,
   Discourse their gaudy wardrobes, plot new pride,
   Jest upon courtiers' legs, laugh at the wagging
   Of their own feathers, and a thousand more
   Delights which private ladies never think of.
   But above all, and wherein thou shalt make
   All other beauties envy thee, the duke,
   The duke himself shall call thee his, and single
   From the fair troop thy person forth to exchange
   Embraces with, lay siege to those soft lips,
   And not remove till he hath suck'd thy heart
   Which, so dissolv'd with thy sweet breath, shall be
   Made part of his, at the same instant he
   Conveying a new soul into thy breast
   With a creating kiss. Why will you
   Appear so ignorant? I speak the dialect
   Of Florence to you. Come, I find your cunning,
   The news does please. The rolling of your eye
   Betrays you, and I see a guilty blush
   Through this white veil upon your cheek. You would
   Have it confirm'd. You shall. The duke himself
   Shall swear he loves you.
   Be not you too peevish now,
   And hinder all our fortune. I ha' promis'd him

To move you for his armful, as I am
Sciarrha, and your brother. More, I ha' sent
Word to him by Lorenzo that you should
Meet his high flame. In plain Italian,
Love him, and command him. Make us.

The Witty Fair One

James Shirley   *Act I, scene iii; Serio-Comic*

Fowler: You would have me praise you, now;
   I could ramble in your commendation. Why,
   You shall hear me.
   Your hairs are Cupid's nets, a forehead like
   The fairest coast of heaven without a cloud,
   Your eyebrow is love's bow, while either eye
   Are arrows drawn to wound; your lips the temple
   Or sacred fane of kisses, often as they meet,
   Exchanging roses.
   Your tongue Love's lightning, neck the milky path
   Or throne where sit the Graces.
   Do not I know that I have abused you all this
While, or do you think I love you a thought the better, or,
with all my poetical daubings, can alter the complexion of a
hair now? No dispraise to you, I have seen as handsome a
woman ride upon a sack to market, that never knew the
impulsion of a coat or the price of a stammel petticoat; and I
have seen a worse face in a countess; what o' that? Must you
be proud because men call you handsome? And yet, though
we are so foolish to tell you so, you might have more wit
than to believe it. Your eyes may be matched, I hope. For
your nose, there be richer in our sex; tis true that you have
color for your hair, we grant it, and for your cheeks, but
what do your teeth stand you in, lady? Your lips are pretty,
but you lay them too open, and men breathe too much upon
them. For your tongue, we all leave you, there's no contest-
ing. Your hand is fine, but your gloves whiter, and for your
leg, if the commendation or goodness of it be in the small,
there be bad enough in gentlemen's stockings to compare
with it. Come, remember you are imperfect creatures without a man. Be not you a goddess; I know you are mortal and

had rather make you my companion than my idol. This is no flattery, now.

The Witty Fair One

James Shirley   *Act II, scene ii; Serio-Comic*

Brains: This whelp has some plot upon me, I smell powder. My young mistress would have blown up my brains. It is not the first time she hath conspired so, but it will not do, I was never yet cozened in my life, and if I pawn my brains for a bottle of sack or claret, may my nose, as a brand for my negligence, carry everlasting malmsey in it, and be studded with rubies and carbuncles! — Mistress, you must pardon my officiousness; be as angry as a tiger, I must play the dragon, and watch your golden fleece. My master has put me in trust, and I am not so easily corrupted. I have but two eyes, Argus has a hundred, but he must be a cunning Mercury must pipe them both asleep, I can tell you. And now I talk of sleep, my lodging is next to her chambers; it is a confidence in my master to let his livery lie so near her; servingmen have ere now proved themselves no eunuchs with their masters' daughters; if I were so lusty as some of my own tribe, it were no great labor to commit burglary upon a maidenhead; but all my nourishment runs upwards, into brains, and I am glad on't. A temperate blood is sign of a good liver. I am past tilting. Here she is, with the second part of her to the same tune, another maid that has a grudging of the green sickness, and wants a man to recover her.

The Wild Gallant

John Dryden   *Act III, scene ii; Serio-Comic*

Loveboy: I have promised my Lady Constance an hundred pounds ere night; I had four hours to perform it in when I engag'd to do it; and I have slept out more than two of them. All my hope to get this money lies within the compass of that hat there. — Before I lay down I made bold a little to prick my finger, and write a note in the blood of it, to this same friend of mine in t'other world, that uses to supply me; the Devil has now had above two hours to perform it in; all which time I have slept to give him the better opportunity: time enough for a Gentleman of his agility to fetch it from the East-Indies, out of one of his Temples where they worship him; or if he were lazy, and not minded to go so far, 'twere but stepping over sea and borrowing so much money, out of his own Bank at Amsterdam! Hang't, what's an hundred pounds between him and me? — Now does my heart go pit a pat, for fear I should not find the money there; I would fain lift it up to see, and yet I am so fraid of missing; yet a plague, why should I fear he'll fail me; the name of friend's a sacred thing; sure he'll consider that. Methinks this Hat looks as if it should have something under it; if one could see the yellow boys peeping underneath the brims, now — ha! In my conscience, I think I do. Stand out of the way, sirrah, and be ready to gather up the pieces that will flush out of the hat as I take it up. [Loveboy snatches up the hat, looks in it hastily, and sees nothing but the Paper] Now the Devil take the Devil. Ah, plague! Was ever man so served as I am? [Throws his hat upon the ground] To break the bonds of Amity for 100 pieces; well, it shall be more out of thy way than thou imaginest, Devil; I'll turn Parson, and be at open defiance with thee; I'll lay the wickedness of all people upon thee, though thou art never so innocent; I'll convert thy Bawds and

Whores; I'll hector thy Gamesters, that they shall not dare to swear, curse, or bubble. Nay, I'll set thee out so, that thy very Usurers and Aldermen shall fear to have do with thee!

Bibliography

Adventures of Five Hours
Sir Samuel Tuke

> *A Select Collection of Old English Plays*, Vol. 15 edited by Robert Dodsley; originally published in 1744

Alcibiades
Thomas Otway

> *The Works of Thomas Otway*, Vol. 1 edited by J.C. Ghosh; Oxford: The Clarendon Press 1932

All Mistaken, or, The Mad Couple
James Howard

> *A Select Collection of Old English Plays*, Vol. 15 edited by Robert Dodsley; originally published in 1744

Amphitryon
John Dryden

> *The Works of John Dryden*, Vol. 15 edited by Earl Miner; Berkeley: University of California Press 1976

> *Dryden: The Dramatic Works* edited by Montague Summers; London: The Nonesuch Press 1932

Antonio's Revenge
John Marston

> *Antonio's Revenge* edited by W. Reavley Gair; Manchester: Manchester University Press/Baltimore: Johns Hopkins University Press 1978

> *Antonio's Revenge* edited by G.K. Hunter; Lincoln: University of Nebraska Press 1965

> *The Plays of John Marston* edited by H. Harvey Wood; Edinburgh, London: Oliver and Boyd 1934

Selected Plays of John Marston edited by MacDonald P. Jackson and Michael Neill; Cambridge: Cambridge University Press 1986

The Brothers
James Shirley

> *The Dramatic Works and Poems of James Shirley, Vol.* 1 edited by William Gifford and Alexander Dyce; London: John Murray 1833

The Cheats
John Wilson

> *The Dramatic Works of John Wilson;* New York: Benjamin Blom 1967

The Choleric Fathers
Thomas Holcroft

> *Plays of Holcroft;* London: G. Robinson 1782

The City Nightcap
Robert Davenport

> *A Select Collection of Old English Plays, Vol.* 13 edited by Robert Dodsley; originally published in 1744
>
> *A Critical Edition of The City Night-Cap* edited by Willis J. Monie; New York: Garland Publishing Company 1979

The Clandestine Marriage
David Garrick and George Colman the Elder

> *The Plays of David Garrick, Vol.* 1 edited by Harry William Pedicord and Frederick Louis Bergmann; Carbondale: University of Illinois Press 1980
>
> *Plays by David Garrick and George Colman the Elder* edited by E.R. Wood; Cambridge: Cambridge University Press 1982

Plays of the Restoration and Eighteenth Century edited by
Dougald MacMillan and Howard Mumford Jones; New York:
Henry Holt and Company 1931

British Plays from the Restoration to 1820 edited by Montrose J.
Moses; Boston: Little Brown and Company 1931

The Constant Couple
George Farquhar

> *The Constant Couple;* London: Methuen Drama 1988
>
> *The Works of George Farquhar* edited by Shirley Strum Kenny;
> Oxford: The Clarendon Press 1988
>
> *The Complete Works of George Farquhar* edited by Charles
> Stonehill; New York: The Gordian Press 1967/London: The
> Nonesuch Press 1930

The Contrast
Royall Tyler

> *The Contrast;* New York: AMS Press 1970

The Critic
Richard Brinsley Sheridan

> *The Critic* edited by David Crane; London: A & C Black/New
> York: W.W. Norton 1989
>
> *British Dramatists from Dryden to Sheridan* edited by George
> H. Nettleton and Arthur E. Case; Boston: Houghton Mifflin
> Company 1939
>
> *Sheridan: Plays* edited by Cecil Price; London: Oxford
> University Press 1975
>
> *The Plays and Poems of Richard Brinsley Sheridan* edited by R.
> Crompton Rhodes; New York: The Macmillan Company 1929

Cure for a Cuckold
John Webster

> *The Works of John Webster, Vol.* 3 edited by F.L. Lucas; London:
> Chatto and Windus 1927

The Discovery
Frances Sheridan

> *The Plays of Frances Sheridan* edited by Robert Hogan and
> Jerry C. Beasley; Newark: University of Delaware Press 1984

The Double Dealer
William Congreve

> *The Double Dealer* edited by J.C. Ross; W.W. Norton, New
> York/Ernest Benn Ltd., London 1981

> *Comedies of William Congreve* edited by Anthony G.
> Henderson; Cambridge University Press 1982

> *Complete Plays of William Congreve* edited by Herbert Davis;
> University of Chicago Press Chicago, London 1967

> *Comedies by Congreve* edited by Bonamy Dobree; Oxford
> University Press, London 1959

> *Complete Works of William Congreve, Vol.* 2 edited by
> Montague Summers; Russell and Russell Inc., New York 1964

The Dutch Courtesan
John Marston

> *Selected Plays of John Marston* edited by MacDonald P. Jackson,
> Michael Neill; Cambridge University Press, Cambridge 1986

> *Plays by John Marston, Vol.* 2 edited by H. Harvey Wood;
> Oliver and Boyd Edinburgh, London 1938

> *The Dutch Courtesan* edited by Peter Davison; University of
> California Press: Berkeley, LA 1968

> *The Works of John Marston* edited by A.H. Bullen; John C.
> Nimmo, London 1888

> *Drama of the English Renaissance Vol* 2: *The Stuart Period* edited
> by Russell A. Fraser and Norman Rabkin; Macmillan
> Publishing Co., New York/Collier Macmillan Publishers,
> London 1976

> *The Dutch Courtesan* edited by M.L. Wine; University of
> Nebraska Press Lincoln 1965

Every Man in His Humor
Ben Jonson

> *Every Man in His Humor* edited by J.W. Lever; Lincoln:
> University of Nebraska Press 1971
>
> *Every Man in His Humor* edited by Gabriele Bernhard Jackson;
> New Haven and London: Yale University Press 1969
>
> *Every Man in His Humor* edited by Martin Seymour-Smith;
> New York: Hill and Wang 1966
>
> *Every Man in His Humor* edited by John Caird; London:
> Methuen London Ltd. 1986
>
> *Ben Jonson, Volume 3* edited by C.H. Herford and Percy
> Simpson; Oxford: The Clarendon Press 1927
>
> *Complete Plays of Ben Jonson, Vol.* 1 edited by G.A. Wilkes,
> based on the edition by Herford and Simpson; Oxford: The
> Clarendon Press 1981

Fatal Curiosity
George Lillo

> *Fatal Curiosity* edited by William H. McBurney; Lincoln:
> University of Nebraska Press 1966

The Fawn
John Marston

> *The Plays of John Marston* edited by H. Harvey Wood;
> Edinburgh, London: Oliver and Boyd 1934
>
> *The Fawn* edited by Gerald A. Smith; Lincoln: University of
> Nebraska Press 1965
>
> *The Fawn* edited by David Blostein; Manchester: University of
> Manchester Press Baltimore: Johns Hopkins University Press
> 1978

The Fleire
Edward Sharpham

> *A Critical Old Spelling Edition of the Works of Edward Sharpham* edited by Christopher Gordon Petter; New York: Garland Publishing Inc. 1986

The Grateful Servant
James Shirley

> *The Dramatic Works and Poems of James Shirley, Vol.* 2 edited by William Gifford and Alexander Dyce; London: John Murray 1833

The Ladies of Castile
Mercy Otis Warren

> *The Plays and Poems of Mercy Otis Warren* edited by Benjamin Franklin V; Delmar (NY): Scholar's Facsimiles and Reprints

The Lady's Last Stake
Colley Cibber

> *The Plays of Colley Cibber, Vol.* 2 edited by Rodney L. Hayley; New York, London: Garland Publishing Inc. 1980

Love for Love
William Congreve

> *Comedies of William Congreve* edited by Anthony G. Henderson; Cambridge: Cambridge University Press 1982

> *Complete Plays of William Congreve* edited by Herbert Davis; Chicago: University of Chicago Press 1967

> *Comedies by Congreve* edited by Bonamy Dobree; London: Oxford University Press 1959

> *Complete Works of William Congreve, Vol.* 2 edited by Montague Summers; New York: Russell and Russell Inc. 1964

> *Love for Love* edited by M.M. Kelsall; London: Ernest Benn Ltd. 1969

Love for Love edited by Emmett L. Avery; Lincoln: University of Nebraska Press 1966

Three Restoration Plays edited by Gamini Salgado; Baltimore: Penguin 1968

Love Tricks
James Shirley

The Dramatic Works of Shirley, Vol. 1 edited by William Gifford and Alexander Dyce; John Murray, London 1833

Love's Contrivance
Susanna Centlivre

The Plays of Susanna Centlivre, Vol. 1 edited by Richard Frushell; New York: Garland Publishing Inc. 1982

The Dramatic Works of Mrs. Susanna Centlivre; London: John Pearson 1872

The Man of Mode
George Etherege

The Man of Mode; London: Methuen London Ltd 1988

The Man of Mode edited by John Barnard; London: Ernest Benn Ltd. New York: W.W. Norton and Co. Inc 1979

The Man of Mode edited by W.B. Carnochan; Lincoln: University of Nebraska 1966

The Plays of Sir George Etherege edited by Michael Cordner; Cambridge: Cambridge University Press 1982

The Minor
Samuel Foote

Plays by Samuel Foote and Arthur Murphy edited by George Taylor; Cambridge: Cambridge University Press 1984

The Mistake
Sir John Vanbrugh

> *Sir John Vanbrugh, Vol.* 2 edited by W.C. Ward; London:
> Lawrence and Bullen 1893

The New Inn
Ben Jonson

> *The New Inn;* London: Methuen London Ltd. 1987

> *Selected Plays of Ben Jonson* edited by Johanna Proctor;
> Cambridge: Cambridge University Press 1989

> *The Complete Plays of Ben Jonson, Vol.* 4 edited by G.A. Wilkes,
> based on the edition edited by C.H. Herford and Evelyn
> Simpson; Oxford: Clarendon Press 1981

The Old Bachelor
William Congreve

> *The Works of William Congreve* edited by Montague Summers;
> New York: Russell and Russell Inc. 1964

> *Comedies of William Congreve edited* by Anthony G.
> Henderson; Cambridge: Cambridge University Press 1982

> *Complete Plays of William Congreve* edited by Herbert Davis;
> Chicago: University of Chicago Press 1967

> *Comedies by Congreve* edited by Bonamy Dobree; London:
> Oxford University Press 1959

The Old Couple
Thomas May

> *A Select Collection of Old English Plays, Vol.* 12 edited by Robert
> Dodsley; originally published in 1744

The Ordinary
William Cartwright

> *A Select Collection of Old English Plays, Vol.* 12 edited by Robert
> Dodsley; originally published in 1744

The Plays and Poems of William Cartwright edited by G. Blakemore Evans; Madison: University of Wisconsin Press 1951

Oroonoko
Thomas Southerne

> *Oroonoko* edited by Maximilian E. Novak and David Stuart Rodes; Lincoln: University of Nebraska Press 1976
>
> *The Works of Thomas Southerne*, Vol. 2 edited by Robert Jordan and Harold Love; Oxford: The Clarendon Press 1988

The Projectors
John Wilson

> *The Dramatic Works of John Wilson* edited by James Maidment and W.H. Logan; Edinburgh: 1874/New York: Benjamin Blom 1967

The Provoked Husband
Sir John Vanbrugh and Colley Cibber

> *The Provoked Husband* edited by Peter Dixon; Lincoln: University of Nebraska Press 1973

The Relapse
Sir John Vanbrugh

> *The Relapse* edited by Curt A. Zimansky; Lincoln: University of Nebraska Press 1970
>
> *The Relapse* edited by Bernard Harris; London: Ernest Benn Ltd. 1971
>
> *British Dramatists from Dryden to Sheridan* edited by George H. Nettleton and Arthur E. Case; Boston: Houghton Mifflin Co. 1939
>
> *Sir John Vanbrugh, Vol.* 1 edited by W.C. Ward; London: Lawrence and Bullen 1893

The Sack of Rome
Mercy Otis Warren

> *The Plays and Poems of Mercy Otis Warren* edited by Benjamin Franklin V; Delmar (NY): Scholar's Facsimiles and Reprints

Sir Courtly Nice
John Crowne

> *The Dramatic Works of John Crowne, Vol. 3;* Edinburgh: 1874/New York: Benjamin Blom 1967

> *Sir Courtly Nice* edited by Charlotte Bradford Hughes; The Hague: Mouton and Co. 1966

> *The Comedies of John Crowne* edited by B.J. McMullin; New York: Garland Publishing Company 1984

The Soldier's Fortune
Thomas Otway

> *The Works of Thomas Otway, Vol. 2* edited by J.C. Ghosh; Oxford: The Clarendon Press 1932

The Traitor
James Shirley

> *The Dramatic Works and Poems of James Shirley, Vol. 2* edited by William Gifford and Alexander Dyce; London: John Murray 1833

> *The Traitor* edited by John Stewart Carter; Lincoln: The University of Nebraska Press 1965

Two Noble Kinsmen
William Shakespeare & John Fletcher

> *Beaumont & Fletcher: Dramatic Works, Vol. 7* edited by Fredson Bowers; Cambridge: Cambridge University Press 1989

> *The Two Noble Kinsmen* edited by Eugene M. Waith; Oxford: The Clarendon Press/New York: Oxford University Press 1989

> *The Two Noble Kinsmen* edited by Clifford Leech; New York: New American Library 1966

The Two Noble Kinsmen; London: Methuen London Ltd 1986

Venice Preserved
Thomas Otway

> *Venice Preserved* edited by Malcolm Kelsall; Lincoln: University of Nebraska Press 1969
>
> *The Works of Thomas Otway, Vol.* 2 edited by J.C. Ghosh; Oxford: The Clarendon Press 1932

The Virtuoso
Thomas Shadwell

> *The Virtuoso* edited by Marjorie Hope Nicolson and David Stuart Rodes; Lincoln: University of Nebraska Press 1966
>
> *The Works of Thomas Shadwell, Vol.* 3 edited by Montague Summers; London: The Fortune Press 1927

The Way of the World
William Congreve

> *The Way of the World* edited by Kathleen Martha Lynch; Lincoln: University of Nebraska Press 1965
>
> *The Way of the World* edited by Brian Gibbons; London: Ernest Benn Ltd. 1971
>
> *Comedies of William Congreve* edited by Anthony G. Henderson; Cambridge University Press 1982
>
> *Complete Plays of William Congreve* edited by Herbert Davis; University of Chicago Press Chicago, London 1967
>
> *Comedies by Congreve* edited by Bonamy Dobree; Oxford University Press, London 1959
>
> *Complete Works of William Congreve, Vol.* 3 edited by Montague Summers; Russell and Russell Inc., New York 1964
>
> *British Dramatists from Dryden to Sheridan* edited by George H. Nettleton and Arthur E. Case; Boston: Houghton Mifflin Co. 1939
>
> *British Plays from the Restoration to* 1820 edited by Montrose J. Moses; Boston: Little Brown and Co. 1931

The Witty Fair One
James Shirley

> *The Dramatic Works and Poems of James Shirley, Vol.* 1 edited by
> William Gifford and Alexander Dyce; London: John Murray
> 1833

The Wild Gallant
John Dryden

> *Dryden: The Dramatic Works, Vol.* 1 edited by Montague
> Summers; London: The Nonesuch Press 1931

> *The Works of John Dryden, Vol.* 8 edited by John Harrington
> Smither and Douglas MacMillan volume editors, Textual editor: Vinton A. Dearing; Berkeley: University of California
> Press 1962